SINGAPORE

The Solo Girl's Travel Guide

TRAVEL ALONE. NOT LONELY.

ALEXA WEST

Copyright © 2020 Alexa West Publishing
All rights reserved

THE SGTG MANTRA

"If you want to live a life you've never lived, you have to do things you've never done."

Every girl should travel solo at least once in her life.
You don't need a boyfriend, a travel partner or anyone's approval to travel the world. And you don't need a massive bank account or an entire summer off work.

All you need is that wanderlust in your blood and a good book in your hands.

If you've doubted yourself for one moment, remember this:

Millions of girls travel across the globe all by themselves every damn day and you can, too.

You are just as capable, just as smart, and just as brave as the rest of us. You don't need permission—this is your life.

Listen to your gut, follow your heart, and just book that ticket already!

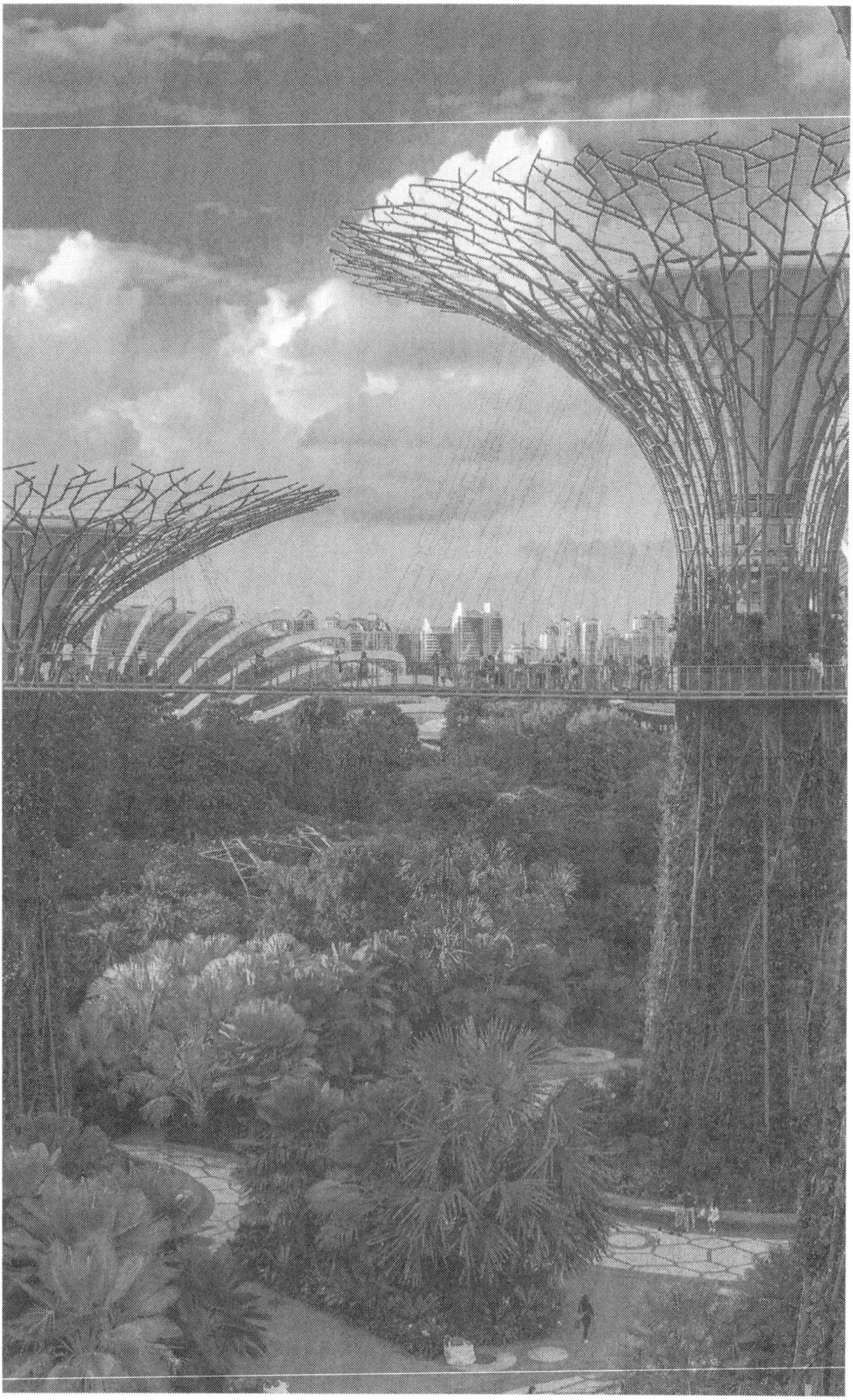

DON'T FORGET YOUR *Map!*

To keep the price of this book affordable for you, there are no fancy color maps inside.

I've got something even better.

Visit the link below to get your interactive map that you can travel with throughout Singapore.

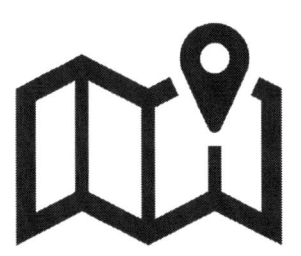

TheSoloGirlsTravelGuide.com/Maps

ABOUT THE AUTHOR

Hey, I'm Alexa.

Back in 2010, I was a broke-ass Seattle girl who had just graduated from college and had about $200 to my name. I was faced with two choices: Get a job, find a husband, and have 3 babies . . . or sell everything I owned, travel the world and disappoint my parents.

Obviously, I made the right choice.

Today, I'm a best-selling author, travel blogger, and female-focused entrepreneur who has been traveling solo across the globe for nearly a decade. And now, I'm using my travel lessons (and mistakes) to change the way that women travel the world.

The Solo Girl's Travel Guide is the #1 best-selling travel guidebook series for women . . . and my baby.

As a self-published author, I can write whatever the hell I want. And I want to write about REAL adventures, involve my local friends, and pave a safe travel path for you.

Follow in my footsteps and let me show you how to do this.

xoxo, Alexa

A LITTLE BIT OF *Honesty*...

I'm not here to get rich or reach 1 million followers on Instagram.

I'm here because I love to travel. And I love to help other girls travel, too. Simple as that.

I started writing The Solo Girl's Travel Guide for my actual friends planning big trips around the world.

All with the goal of showing them how to travel in a short amount of time on a realistic budget.

And now, I write this book for you.

So! A true Singapore vacation should be equal amounts street food, temple hopping, and nightlife. And that's exactly what this guide is.

What this Guide is not . . .

✘ An overwhelming deep-dive into Singapore's history

✘ An 8-hour read with historical dates and ancient facts

✘ A book written by some man who just doesn't get it . . .

Speaking of men, since the success of The Solo Girl's Travel Guide, I've had many dudes ask me, "Yeah, but why a girl's guide?"

Um, because we have breasts. And for some reason, that's enough for the world to treat us like toys. We constantly have to ask ourselves questions like . . .

Ω Are there drugs in my drink?

Ω Is that dark alley filled with serial killers?

Ω Am I going to be kidnapped and sold to the highest bidder?

The answer is usually NO, but for us girls, "usually" doesn't cut it. In order to be wild and carefree, we've got to feel 100% safe. And I've never found a travel guide to take my safety into consideration . . . so, here we are.

Go into your vacation knowing that I'm leading you to the BEST, the SAFEST, and the TOTALLY WORTH it spots. Let your hair down and tell your mom not to worry. I've got you.

So, as we get into this guide—I want to make a few promises to you:

Ω I won't bullshit you and tell you that a beach is awesome if it's not.

Ω I will tell you what spots are worth your time—and what spots to skip.

Ω And I will make planning this vacation so easy and so fun!!!

Your bags may not be packed, but your vacation officially starts now.

Oh, and once you've bought this book . . . we're officially friends. I'm here if you need me. Just write me on Instagram @SoloGirlsTravelGuide

Let's go to Singapore!

TABLE OF CONTENTS

Top 10 Singapore Experiences 1
Top 10 Singapore Food Spots 2
Intro to Singapore 3
A Mental Map of Singapore 5
Weather in Singapore 8

SINGAPORE SURVIVAL GUIDE 10

From the Airport 11
Transportation in Singapore 13
How to Budget for Singapore 15
Pro Money Tips for Singapore 17
Sim Cards + Local Apps 18
Local Apps to Download 20
Dating in Singapore 23
Alexa's Pro Tips for Singapore 24
Singapore Food Guide 26

CHAPTER 1 : MARINA BAY 29

Where to Stay in Marina Bay 30
Where to Eat in Marina Bay 32
What to Do in Marina Bay 37

Where to Shop in Marina Bay 39

CHAPTER 2 : CHINATOWN 40

Streets to Explore in Chinatown. 41
Where to Stay in Chinatown. 43
Where to Eat in Chinatown 49
What to Do in Chinatown. 53

CHAPTER 3 : KAMPONG GLAM 56

The Hipster Hood. 56
Where to Stay in Kampong Glam 57
Where to Eat in Kampong Glam 64
What to Do in Kampong Glam. 67
Shopping in Kampong Glam 70

CHAPTER 4 : LITTLE INDIA 72

Where to Stay 74
Where to Eat in Little India. 78
What to Do in Little India. 81
Shopping in Little India 83

CHAPTER 5: CENTRAL BUSINESS DISTRICT: ANYTHING BUT STRICTLY BUSINESS 85

Where to Stay in the CBD. 86
Where to Eat in the CBD. 91
What to Do in the CBD. 96
Shopping in the CBD 97

CHAPTER 6: OTHER PLACES IN SINGAPORE 98

CHAPTER 7: NIGHTLIFE IN SINGAPORE............................107

CHAPTER 8: CHANGI AIRPORT....................................110
    How to Get to the Airport...111
    Where to Eat in the Airport 112
    Things to do in Changi Airport 114
    Where to Sleep in Changi Airport 117

    Itineraries for Singapore..121

PREPPING FOR SINGAPORE 127
    Visas..128
    Packing List for Singapore 133
    Festivals and Holidays in Singapore 135
    Directory 138
    The True Story..140

Gardens by the Bay

TOP 10 SINGAPORE
Experiences

1. Gardens by the Bay
2. Singapore Flyer
3. Eat at a hawker enter
4. Singapore River Cruise
5. Eat in Little India
6. Take a Free Walking Tour
7. Boon Tat Street at 6:57pm
8. Explore Changi Airport & Jewel
9. Eat an Entire Meal at 7-Eleven
10. Swim in Marina Bay Sands' infinity pool

TOP 10 SINGAPORE
Food Spots

1. Maxwell Food Centre
2. Chinatown Hawker Centre
3. Boon Tat Street at 6:57pm
4. Lao Pa Sat
5. Din Tai Fung
6. Newton Hawker Centre
7. Makansutra Gluttons Bay
8. East Coast Seafood Centre
9. Tiong Bahru Market for breakfast
10. Liao Fan Hawker Chan - Singapore's famous Michelin restaurant

INTRO TO

SINGAPORE

There is truly no place like Singapore. It's one of the smallest countries in the world (just a little bit bigger than Manhattan!), but one of the most diverse countries, too.

Language: English
Population: 5.612 million
Currency: Singapore Dollars $
Crime Rate: One of the lowest in the world

Full of art, luxury, culture, and some of the best food in Asia – Singapore is incredibly futuristic and also incredibly steeped in tradition. From the insane wealth and modernization displayed in Marina Bay to the colorful streets of Little India – a trip to Singapore offers you the opportunity to dive into multiple worlds within one single day.

Did I mention that Singapore is one of the safest countries in the world, too? Solo female travelers - get your walking shoes on, come hungry and get ready to explore one of the most fascinating countries in the world.

THE PEOPLE

The population in Singapore is a fascinating mix of Asian backgrounds – with a heavy majority represented by Chinese, Malaysian and Indian heritage. As a result, diversity is celebrated and Singaporeans are generally really welcoming and inclusive.

THE FOOD

The diverse population in Singapore means there is a diverse food culture in Singapore! Singaporeans take pride in their food - it's an incredible display of the melting pot of cultures that make up Singapore, with different flavors inspired by China, India, and Singapore's Southeast Asian neighbors. Singaporean food is best found at hawker centers. Food hawker centers are a massive part of Singapore's food culture. These are essentially grandiose food courts with hundreds of stalls representing every food culture in Singapore. This is the cheapest way to eat in Singapore, too.

THE RELIGION

Another result of the blended Singaporean culture is that nearly every major religion is represented on this island. The most popular religions are Buddhism, Islam, Christianity, and Hinduism. Because of this variety of culture, there are loads of religious holidays and different temples throughout Singapore!

THE VOLTAGE

Singapore's standard voltage is 230 Volts and the frequency is 50 Hz. This means that if you're from the UK, you'll be fine bringing and using your chargers and appliances with no adapter! If you're from the US, you'll need to find an adapter. For bigger appliances, like hair tools, you'll need a converter - but honestly? With the humidity, I wouldn't even bother trying to straighten or curl your hair.

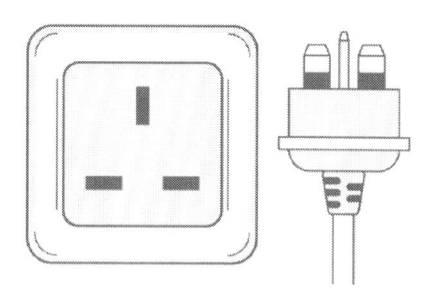

Got all that? Cool. Let's get planning, baby!

A MENTAL MAP OF SINGAPORE
WITH THE HELP OF AN ACTUAL MAP...

*CHAPTER NUMBERS

Singapore is a super compact city and country. The island is organized by neighborhoods, each with their own distinct style and personality. Here are the neighborhoods that will be most relevant to your Singaporean adventure!

MARINA BAY

Marina Bay is what most tourists would consider the heart & center of Singapore. This is where you'll find all of the touristy attractions and Singapore's lap of luxury!

CHINATOWN

Chinatown lies east of Marina Bay and like all respectable Chinatowns around the world...here is where you'll find the best food! Plus, Buddhist temples, museums and unique shopping.

TIONG BAHRU

Wander down south you'll arrive in Tiong Bahru, an incredible residential area known for street art and quirky shops.

CENTRAL BUSINESS DISTRICT

Home to the backbone of Singapore's economy; you'll find tons of skyscrapers and bougie restaurants catering to the international collection of workers.

CLARKE QUAY

Just west of the central business district is Clarke Quay, Singapore's nightlife and party area. It can be quite dull during the daytime, but at night, the area transforms into the best place to spend an evening partying. Just be prepared: nights out can get expensive FAST.

KAMPONG GLAM/BUGIS

Head northeast and check out Kampong Glam and Bugis, Singapore's trendiest neighborhood. This area is best known for the Sultan Mosque, Haji Lane's boutiques, and the tastes of Arab Street.

LITTLE INDIA

Little India is nestled northwest of Kampong Glam and nearly simulates travelling to India. The streets are vibrant, with colorful storefronts, the smells of sweet mangos and freshly cooked food. This is a high-energy neighborhood that's definitely worth a visit.

ORCHARD

Shopping time! If you need to buy anything in Singapore, Orchard is your area with tons of malls and shopping centers. Fair warning: it's VERY easy (and fun) to get lost in a sea of shops.

SENTOSA

After a fee days of city life, you'll need some time to relax! Sentosa's here for that. This is where Singapore's best beaches are hiding, as well as - Universal Studios!

TOP 5 NEIGHBORHOODS TO STAY

1. Marina Bay
2. Central Business District
3. Chinatown
4. Kampong Glam
5. Little India

• •

For more tips, articles, and packing guides—visit my blog at
▶ TheSoloGirlsTravelGuide.com

WEATHER IN Singapore

Singapore is hot and humid year-round, with temperatures ranging from 26°C / 79°F to about 33°C / 91.4°F. Since Singapore is so close to the equator, there isn't much variation in temperature, hours of sunlight, or humidity. There is no winter here!

Speaking of humidity, the humidity in Singapore is usually around 75-90%! Humidity is highest in the morning and then dips down in the afternoon. You'll feel hot, sticky, and your hair will probably go in all sorts of directions. Luckily, air conditioning is EVERYWHERE in Singapore.

November through January are Singapore's wettest months. Expect it to rain pretty much every day. The good news is, however, that Singapore's rain showers are typically fast and exciting downpours. Run for cover when the rain comes! It's the perfect opportunity to duck inside a coffee shop for a quick caffeine fix and water show! After about thirty minutes, most storms let up, the sun reemerges, and you can continue exploring outside in the sunshine.

The rest of the year - February through October - is mostly sunny and clear skies! February through April is considered the official dry season. While you won't get daily downpours, you can expect short bursts of rain every so often.

But really! There's so little variation in Singapore's weather – that you don't need to plan your trip around the weather. Just come.

To summarize:

- ▶ **February - May**
  - Coolest temperatures
  - Least rain
- ▶ **June - October**
  - Warmest temperatures
  - Less rain
- ▶ **November - January**
  - Cooler temperatures
  - Most rain

🕐 WHEN TO VISIT & WHERE

Official Best Time to Visit: February through April
Alexa's Best Time to Visit: Year-Round

☞ FUN FACT

Singapore has one of the highest rates of lightning activity in the world.

SINGAPORE
Survival Guide

- From the Airport 11
- Transportation in Singapore 13
- How to Budget for Singapore 15
- Sim Cards & Local Apps 18
- Do's and Don'ts in Singapore 21
- Dating in Singapore 23
- Alexa's Pro Tips for Singapore 24
- Singapore Food Guide 26

FROM THE *Airport*

Welcome to Singapore! Changi Airport is very well-connected to the city, offering multiple options to get from the airport into the city; options that fit every level of comfort and budget!

OPTION 1: MRT

The cheapest way to travel out of the airport!

The MRT is Singapore's most efficient public transportation system. Trains come every couple of minutes and can get you where you need to go for a low cost.

📍 **Destination:** Bugis, the Central Business District (direct transfer); Orchard, Chinatown, Clarke Quay, and Marina Bay (one connection).

🌐 **Where:** Terminal 2. Follow signs for "trains to city." You can walk between terminals 1, 2, and 3, or you can take the free skytrain between terminals. If you're in terminal 4 or Jewel, you'll need to take the free shuttle bus.

💰 **How Much:** The price of your ticket varies depending on your destination. Expect to pay around $2.

Times of Operation: the earliest train is at 5:31 on Mondays through Saturday. Sunday and public holidays, the earliest train is at 5:59. The latest train is at 11:18.

OPTION 2: METERED TAXI

Whilst more expensive than taking the MRT, the standard, metered taxi is the most convenient and hassle-free way of getting to your destination.

⚑ Destination: Anywhere!

⊕ Where: There are taxi queues at each terminal. The queues can look long but they movie super quickly!

💰 How Much: Expect to pay around $30-35 to the center of Singapore. If you're taking a taxi between midnight and 6am, you'll pay a 50% surcharge of the metered fare. If you're taking a taxi during peak hours (6 am - 9:30 am weekdays, and 6pm to midnight on weekends), expect to pay a 25% surcharge...which leads me to my preferred way of transport in Option 3...

OPTION 3: GRAB

Grab is a rideshare app like Uber. Use the airport's WIFI or purchase a SIM card when you land – then order a GrabTaxi into the city.

⊕ Where: The downside to using a rideshare app is that they can't pick you up right outside the terminal like a taxi would. You'll have to walk to the arrivals pick up point and specify which terminal you're into the driver.

💰 How Much: These are roughly $20-$30 to the central part of Singapore.

☞ **FUN FACT**

Tipping is NOT expected in Singapore but rounding up on taxi fare is appreciated.

Transportation IN SINGAPORE

MRT

The MRT is Singapore's high-speed train public transport. You can get to most tourist destinations with just one or two connections. Trains come every 3 to 6 minutes, which makes the MRT a smart option for exploring Singapore.

▶ MRT TICKETING

Tickets are sold point-to-point in each station. To buy a ticket, go to the ticket machines in the MRT station and enter your destination.

If you're staying in Singapore for more than a few days, I recommend getting an EZ link card. It's a smart card that will save you time, as you can just tap in and out at the station entrances/exits, instead of buying a ticket each time you want to go somewhere. You can buy the EZ link card at most MRT stations, from the person in the ticketing booth. The card costs $12 and comes with $7 in ticket value (so essentially, the card costs $5). Once you use up some money, and have roughly $3 left on the card, you'll have to 'top up' your card. To do this, just go to a ticket machine and add money to your EZ link card.

At the end of your trip, you can refund your card, which gives you your $5 back. You can refund your EZ link card at most MRT stations, at the ticketing booth.

NEED TO KNOW STOPS

- ✓ Changi - the airport
- ✓ Marina Bay - the Marina Bay Mall
- ✓ City Hall / Raffles Place - the central business district
- ✓ Chinatown - Chinatown
- ✓ Harborfront - Sentosa
- ✓ Orchard - ION Orchard Mall
- ✓ Bugis - Bugis Mall
- ✓ Clarke Quay - Clarke Quay

BUS

Singapore's buses cover a pretty extensive amount of Singapore. Check when the bus is scheduled to arrive at your stop, or you could end up waiting for around 30 minutes for the next one. Buy your bus ticket when you get onboard. You can pay with the EZ link card or contactless Mastercard or Visa credit card. To do this, just tap your card at the readers.

If you want to pay by cash, you'll have to have exact change, which requires knowing the stop you're getting off at. I would try to go the contactless route, if possible!

TAXIS

Taxis in Singapore are relatively affordable - you won't be paying as much as you would for a taxi in London or New York City – but they are still the most expensive option. $5-$10 here and there really adds up – especially when you're not sure how far you're driving or how much your final fare will be!

GRAB

Grab is a ridesharing app like Uber. Usually, a GrabTaxi costs around the same price as taxis – but sometimes cheaper. I prefer to take a Grab so I can keep track of my spending. When your Grab car shows up to pick you up, it might be a regular car or it might be an actual taxi car.

WALK

Singapore is a wonderfully walkable city with paved sidewalks and cars that actually obey traffic laws! The city is so walkable, in fact, that I highly recommend going on a free walking tour through Chinatown, Little India, Kampong Glam and more. Check out IndieSingapore.com or MonsterDayTours.com to sign up for your walking tour!

HOW TO *Budget* FOR SINGAPORE

Singapore is known for being an expensive city, comparable to New York. But just like any big city, you can be a bougie bitch by popping bottles in the penthouse suite...but you can also be that low-key traveler who using local tips and tricks to spend wisely. Lemme' break down your spending options.

💰 BUDGET
Hostels, hawker center meals, and a mix of walking and public transport is the way to go!

💰 BALANCED
Stay in a private room or hotel but eat locally! OR flip it around; stay in a hostel but visit a few rooftop bars and beachfront clubs.

💰 BOUGIE
Singapore is THE place to be bougie. With insane luxury hotels, wild nightlife, and Michelin restaurants left and right, get out that credit card! .

	Budget	Balanced	Bougie
Total Per Day	$60	$150	$300

DAILY EXPENSES

Cost	Price in USD
Hawker Center Meal	$6
Restaurant Meal	$30
Hamburger	$19
Bottle of Beer (from a supermarket)	$3
Bottle of Beer (from a bar)	$11
Cocktail	$17
1 Night in a Hostel	$30
1 Night in a Private Room	$120
1 Night in a Resort	$170 +
Day Tour	$60

> ☞ **FUN FACT**
> 17% of the population has an asset worth 1 million dollars or more - that's a LOT of millionaires.

TIPS TO SPEND LESS IN SINGAPORE

▶ Eat at hawker centers - this is where you'll find the cheapest and yummiest local food! Hawker centers are basically gourmet food courts filled with local food stalls (No McDonalds here, babe). Also, don't forget to try the fridge section in 7-Eleven.

▶ Take the MRT and save cabs for nights out, when public transport is closed.

▶ Bring a water bottle to fill up - tap water is safe to drink!

▶ Go shopping in Little India or Chinatown for the most affordable souvenirs

▶ Avoid bars and clubs - drinks are expensive! Do what I do...add tequila to your juice bottle and walk around Marina Bay in the evening. #NoShame

PRO MONEY TIPS FOR SINGAPORE

▶ You need cash. Especially in hawker centers where you can usually only pay with cash.

▶ Bring $75 USD (or your currency equivalent) and exchange this at the airport when you land. That should be enough for hawker centers, street shopping and incidentals in-between (for at least 2-3 days).

▶ After that, take cash out of the ATMs but beware of your bank's exchange fees. I use Charles Schwab which doesn't charge me for using foreign ATMs and they give me a fabulous international exchange rate.

▶ Hotels, restaurants, and shopping centers accept credit cards.

▶ Make sure you're using a credit card that doesn't charge insane international fees - the Chase Sapphire Card and Bank of America Travel Rewards Card don't charge extra for transactions abroad. You'll also want a debit card that doesn't charge international fees to take out cash – I use Charles Schwab.

▶ Connect your debit card to your Grab App now, before you come to Singapore.

SIM CARDS + Local Apps

There are three main mobile service providers in Singapore: Starhub, M1, and Singtel. Each of these providers offer a tourist SIM card, which connects you to data for a cheap price! And with Singapore being such an app-connected city, having data is a MUST in my book! Literally.

STARHUB

This tourist SIM card is called the Travel Prepaid SIM. You pay $12 up front and receive a SIM card valid for 7 days, with 100GB of data, 500 call minutes, and 100 texts. This should be more than enough for a week. Staying longer than 1 week? StarHub offers longer tourist plans, too.

SINGTEL

This tourist SIM card is called the hi!Tourist SIM Card. It is $15 and you receive 100 GB of data, 500 minutes, and 1 GB of roaming data in Australia, Malaysia, Indonesia, and/or Thailand. You also receive unlimited data on Facebook, LINE, WhatsApp, and WeChat.

M1

This SIM card is similar to the others, offering 100 GB of data, 500 minutes of local calls, 100 texts, and 20 minutes of international calls. It's valid for 7 days and there are discounts if you are staying for longer. This costs $12...but M1 stores are a little harder to come by than Starhub and Singtel.

ALEXA'S VOTE FOR THE BEST SIM CARD

The one you see first. Purchase the first one that comes along.

WHERE TO BUY THE SIM CARD

At the Airport: You can buy SIM cards in all terminals. Look for Changi Recommends booths, Starhub stores, Travelers, or Cheers. There are stores inside the terminals, as well as in the arrivals halls.

In the City: You can buy SIM cards from Singtel, Starhub, and M1 stores, as well as some 7/11s. These stores can be found in pretty much every mall, but if you don't know where to go, ION Orchard is a good starting point.

> ☞ **PRO TIP**
> You'll need your passport to buy a SIM card!

LOCAL APPS TO DOWNLOAD

WHATSAPP

The most popular messaging app that allows messaging, calls, and video calls. Local businesses will usually provide their WhatsApp as a point of contact. Download that shit.

MAPS.ME

This is my favorite offline map. Download the Singapore map beforehand you travel.

GRAB

Grab is like Uber, but even cheaper! As a solo female traveler, I'm a huge proponent of ride share apps vs. street taxis. You can identify your driver, track your route, and not get ripped off (even though getting ripped off by taxi drivers is not a thing here in Singapore). Overall, as a general rule of thumb for travel – go with the rideshare app.

SG BUSES

Buses in Singapore are convenient, but some buses only come once every half hour, so this is a good app to have. It tells you when the next bus is coming, so you can plan your route with good connections.

Do's and Don'ts IN SINGAPORE

DO

DO OBEY SINGAPORE'S LAWS

This section is about Singapore's laws! If you haven't already heard, Singapore has very strict laws about very strange things. Here are a few to know to keep you out of trouble...

DO FLUSH THE TOILET

It's against the law to not flush the toilet. While not common, authorities have monitored public restrooms in the past to enforce this rule. Plus, it's just common courtesy.

DON'T

DON'T CHEW GUM

Yep, in an effort to keep Singapore's streets clean and gum-free - gum isn't sold in Singapore.
Punishment for selling chewing gum can result in up to $100,000 in fines or up to 2 years in prison.

DON'T SMOKE

Another effort to keep Singapore's streets sparkly clean - but also, their atmosphere. The act of smoking isn't illegal, but good luck trying to find a place to smoke. Not in the restaurants, not in public spaces, not at the metro stop, not in any indoor area such as markets or metros...the only place to smoke, really, is your own home (which you ain't got).

DON'T LITTER

After reading the previous two, this should come as no surpise. Singapore is extremely clean and it shall stay that way. Throw your trash on the ground and not only are you facing a $300 fine - but also disgust from locals who may just call you out.

DON'T SPIT ON THE GROUND

It's not really a thing that I see many girls doing...but I'll just put this here. Spitting on the ground can cost you up to $1000. I'd assume the same with puking after drinking too much...that one can be a girl thing... find a trash can.

DO ANY KINDS OF DRUGS

No weed, no ecstacy, no mushrooms, even no Adderall - just don't fuck with Singapore's drug laws. I mention this one because in surrounding countries like Thailand or Cambodia...drugs like these can be found on the party islands - but are a big 'no no' in Singapore. I find that many travelers caught with drugs in Asia are almost on autopilot, not realizing that the laws are very different from country to country in southeast asia.

☞ FUN FACT

Airbnbs are illegal in Singapore, but they're often still listed on the site. I recommend avoiding them and staying in a hotel. But if you DO stay in an Airbnb, just keep a low profile. These rules exist so that residential buildings aren't turned into hotels. If you're "caught" you won't get in trouble, but the host will be reprimanded.

Dating IN SINGAPORE

Singapore is an expat island! With a booming finance industry and thriving shipping industry, the island is home to over 1 million expats (aka people who have moved from countries around the world to live and work in Singapore). Translation: you've got heaps of young, single, successful men who'd love to take you out.

Get on Bumble. Get on Tinder. Expect to find a happy hour in Marina Bay or live music in Chinatown.

While Singapore is one of the safest metropolises in the world, still use your judgement.

Ps. Yes, I kind of feel like I'm pimping you out while I'm writing this section.

• •

For more tips, articles, and packing guides—visit my blog at
▶ **TheSoloGirlsTravelGuide.com**

ALEXA'S *Pro Tips* FOR SINGAPORE

♥ ALCOHOL HOURS

After 10:30, you can't drink in public or buy alcohol in supermarkets or shops (including 7/11). You'll have to migrate over to a bar or club, but drinks are significantly more expensive here.

♥ CARRY A LITTLE CASH!

While most shops and restaurants will take card, it's important to carry around a bit of cash. The majority of hawker centers only take cash, and few taxis accept credit card.

♥ "CHOPE" YOUR TABLE

During peak hours, hawker centers get packed – making it hard to find a seat to eat. So, "chope" your table or reserve your seat, by placing a packet of tissues on the seat/stool while you stand in line for your food.

♥ SIT WITH OTHERS

Also, don't be afraid to join an occupied table in a hawker center. It's standard practice.

♥ TAKE ADVANTAGE OF LADIES' NIGHT!

Wednesday nights are Singapore's unofficial ladies' nights, when clubs offer free entry to women (and usually a few drinks, too!). Other nights of the week, these clubs are usually around $30 for entry, so this is a big save. You can also sometimes get free entry by looking up the club on Facebook, finding their events, and message them asking to get on the guest list.

♥ SHIFT CHANGE!

Around 3:30-5 pm, and around 2-4 am, you'll see a 'shift change' sign flashing from quite a few taxis. This means that they're swapping drivers and they'll only go to certain areas of Singapore. You'll have to go up to the window and tell them the general area you want to go to (Orchard, Bugis, Marina Bay, etc.), and they'll either take you or tell you to move onto the next taxi. You'll have to keep asking until a taxi driver is going to the same area as you.

♥ CHEAPER ATTRACTION TICKETS

If you're planning on doing quite a few of the touristy things in Singapore, like the Flyer (huge ferris wheel similar to the London eye), the Night Safari, and Gardens by the Bay, for example, go to Lucky Plaza on Orchard Road. Here, you'll find tour booths that sell bundles of attraction tickets for a better price.

♥ QUICK SNACKS!

Fruit stalls are my go-to! Every hawker center and most malls will have a fruit stall, where you can buy pre-cut fruit (including mango, papaya, and dragon fruit - my favorites!) or have it blended into a fruit juice.

SINGAPORE
Food Guide

Singapore's best local food can be found in hawker centers!

REAL QUICK, LET ME EXPLAIN THE CONCEPT OF HAWKER CENTERS TO YOU.

Hawker Centers are like large garages filled with hundreds of food stalls. Each food stall is typically run by one family who sells a VERY small selection of dishes (sometimes just one dish only) which they have been perfecting for decades. Each owner knows where to source the BEST ingredients for that dish, they stew/steam/bake/broil their fare for hours and start prepping their dishes often before the sun even comes up. So, when you arrive – you are getting a fresh, specialized, gourmet plate of food that that family has mastered...all for prices cheaper than you can imagine.

▶ **CHICKEN RICE**

This is Singapore's unofficial national dish. Poached chicken with rice cooked in chicken stock. It's served with soup. Simple, but absolutely delicious.

▶ **BAK KUT TEH**

The most flavorful pork rib soup. One of my favorite dishes when I want something light to eat.

▶ **CHAR KWAY TEOW**

The most flavorful pork rib soup. One of my favorite dishes when I want something light to eat.

▶ **BAK CHOR MEE**

Flat noodles with minced meat and a vinegar-based sauce.

▶ **CHILI CRAB**

Crab cooked in a spicy, sweet, and savory chili and tomato sauce. This is a must-try in Singapore!

▶ **SATAY**

Skewered and grilled meat served with a peanut sauce. Hit up Lau Pa Sat at 7pm to try the best satay in Singapore.

▶ **LAKSA**

A spicy coconut-based soup served with noodles and traditionally, seafood.

▶ **MURTABAK**

A thin roti or crepe-like pancake stuffed with meat, veggies, or other fillings.

▶ **NASI LEMAK**

Coconut rice with fried meat, a boiled egg, and small fried anchovies.

▶ **SAMBAL STINGRAY**

Stingray grilled in a banana leaf and slathered with sambal, a spicy chili sauce.

▶ **CENDOL**

A super sweet dessert made up of ribbons of green rice flour jelly, coconut milk, and palm sugar syrup.

▶ **KAYA TOAST**

A big slab of butter and kaya plus, a sweet, egg-based, coconut custard jam - slathered between two slices of toast.

▶ **MANGO MILK ICE**

Shaved ice layered with condensed milk and mango.

chicken rice

*Okay, enough of big sister mode.
Let's get to the fun stuff!*

CHAPTER ONE

Marina Bay

THE MOST LUXURIOUS DISTRICT IN SINGAPORE

From the glamourous infinity rooftop pool of Marina Bay Sands to the futuristic supertrees of Gardens by the Bay, Singapore's iconic stamp of luxury starts here. Marina Bay is considered the heart of Singapore with some of the most lavish hotels the waterfront and a Louis Vuitton island store floating in the bay. Whether you're looking to see Singapore's most famous sights or to splash out some serious cash, come wander (or stay) in Marina Bay.

WHERE TO STAY IN MARINA BAY

It's no surprise that the hotels in Marina Bay are pricey! Hotels here start at around $250 per night and are worth every penny for the glam experience.

THE FULLERTON HOTEL

The Fullerton Hotel was built in 1928 under British colonialism. It's a historical building that used to house the General Post Office, the Exchange, the Singapore Club, and various government departments. Today, this beautiful building is a luxury hotel with a glittering view of Marina Bay.

💰 **Starts at:** $307 SGD/ $225 USD

🌐 **Where:** Where the Singapore River meets Marina Bay

🌐 **Address:** 1 Fullerton Square

MANDARIN ORIENTAL

Hello, Sexy. The Mandarin Oriental borders Marina Bay and the Central Business District –providing amazing views of Marina Bay, while also being close to the city center. Peer out your hotel window for a sparkling views of Singapore's city skyline. Jump in the pool and get a vista of Marina Bay. Head outside the lobby doors and you're transported to Sex and The City vibes immediately.

💰 **Starts at:** $359 SGD/ $263 USD

🌐 **Where:** In between Marina Bay and the North Central Business District.

🌐 **Address:** 5 Raffles Avenue

THE RITZ CARLTON

Don't we all want to stay at The Ritz Carlton just once in our lives? This opulent hotel rests on the edge of Marina Bay, offering views of both the skyscrapers of the Central Business District and the Marina Bay Sands (perfect to watch the light show every evening). The best part of this hotel, though, is the bathrooms! Some of the nicer rooms have bathtubs with a large window overlooking Singapore's skyline. Sign me up!

💰 **Starts at:** $459 SGD / $336 USD

🌐 **Where:** Marina Bay, near the Singapore Flyer

🌐 **Address:** 7 Raffles Avenue

MARINA BAY SANDS

Marina Bay Sands (also called MBS by the locals) is the symbol of Singapore, with its image plastered all over book covers, YouTube thumbnails, and post cards! This three-towered hotel is home to a casino, a mall, a night club (MARQUEE), and one of the most famous infinity pools in the world – sitting on the 57th rooftop level – overlooking the entire bay. Only guests can swim in the pool with one of the greatest views of Singapore, so staying at this exclusive hotel is a bucket list item for sure!

💰 **Starts at:** $439 SGD / $322 USD

🌐 **Where** The heart of Marina Bay, close to Gardens by the Bay

🌐 **Address:** 10 Bayfront Avenue

THE FULLERTON BAY HOTEL

The Fullerton Bay Hotel is a modern hotel inside a historical building whose architecture preserves elements of old colonial Singapore. This is another luxury hotel, that arguably has better views than Marina Bay Sands as it's positioned on the opposite side of the bay from the MBS – giving you an incredible view of the bay AND the MBS (did ya get all that?). The rooftop bar, while pricy, is a fantastic place to end your day - again, with a great view!

💰 **Starts at:** $632 SGD / $463 USD

🌐 **Where:** The heart of Marina Bay, close to the city

🌐 **Address:** 80 Collyer Quay

WHERE TO EAT IN MARINA BAY

♥ BUDGET EATS

For cheap eats in Marina Bay, hawker centers and food courts are inexpensive places with so much variety! From Chinese to Malaysian to Thai or Indian – you can eat a filling lunch for as low as $4. When in doubt, go for chicken rice!

MAKANSUTRA GLUTTONS BAY

Cheap food with a pretty spectacular view. Makansutra Gluttons Bay is a local experience.
It's loud, it's casual, and it's delicious. Seafood is this hawker center's specialty. If you're trying to save money, skip buying a fish by the pound and go for a rice or noodle-based dish with shrimp!

⊙ **Open:** 5 pm - 2 am M-Th, 5 pm - 3 am Fr-Sat, 4 pm - 1 am Sundays

⊕ **Address:** 8 Raffles Ave, 15 Esplanade

MARINA SQUARE MALL

For a balance of western food and Asian food. The Marina Square food court is one of the best food court gems near Marina Bay AND…one of the less crowded ones. Like most mall food courts, this place has everything from Bubble Tea to burgers.

⊙ **Open:** 10 am – 10 pm

⊕ **Address:** 6 Raffles Blvd

SUNTEC CITY MALL

A great stop if you're on your way towards the central business district. The food court in Suntec City is called Food Republic and the chicken rice and duck rice stalls are my favorites!

⊙ **Open:** 7 am - 10 pm on weekdays, 8:30 am - 10 pm on weekends

⊕ **Address:** B1 level of Suntec City, 3 Temasek Blvd, Singapore 038983

♥ MID-RANGE EATS

With a mid-ranged budget, you have quite a few more options when it comes to food in Marina Bay. Here are some of my favorites!

OVEREASY

After a week of noodles, sometimes all you want is a good burger. OverEasy is Singapore's version of an American diner where French Fries and Coca Cola are the name of the game. If you can, grab a seat outside to get the best view of Marina Bay! Heads up: on weekends, this place is incredibly lively, with beer pong and groups of people in their 20s or 30s having a boozy night out.

⊙ **Open:** 11:30 am - 11 pm M-Tue, 11:30 am - 1 am W-Sat, 11 am - 11 pm Sun

⊕ **Address:** 1 Fullerton Road

TIM HO WAN

Tim Ho Wan is a Michelin star restaurant with casual dining prices. Their dim sum is excellent - traditional and simple, yet elevated. This place is known for their baked BBQ pork buns and their shrimp rice rolls. Order a few dishes to share...or just do what I do and plan to take half the food home for a late-night snack.

⊙ **Open:** 10:30 am - 10 pm

⊕ **Address:** B2-02 in The Shoppes at Marina Bay

LEVEL 33

This restaurant is split into three sections - the dining room, the social, and the terrace. The dining room is expensive, but the social and the

MARINA BAY 33

terrace are much more affordable. This is a great place for craft beers with a view! The terrace is an outdoor space with a vista of the bay.

Open: 11:30 am - 12 am M-Th, 11:30am - 2 am F-Sat, 12pm - 12 am Sun

Address: 8 Marina Boulevard, Tower 1

PASARBELLA

Pasarbella is an upscale food center. Like a hawker center, it's made up of a bunch of different stalls with shared seating, but these stalls are often individual restaurants with international cuisine like burgers, pho and sushi!

Open: 10 am - 10 pm

Address: Suntec City, 3 Temasek Blvd - North Wing

VATOS URBAN TACOS

Vatos Urban Tacos is a regular go-to of mine. It's known for Korean-Mexican fusion done in the best way. I love the pork tacos and the kimchi fries. The flavor combinations are unexpected but executed brilliantly. I'm drooling just thinking about it.

Open: 5:30 - 11 pm Mon, 12 - 11 pm Tue-Th, 12 pm - 12 am F-Sat, 12 - 11 pm Sun

Address: 36 Beach Road

♥ LUXURY EATS

Fine-dining is half the hype in Singapore's luxury scene. Marina Bay has a wide range of luxury dining options, and there are quite a few celebrity chef restaurants that are well-loved in the area.

SPAGO DINING ROOM BY WOLFGANG PUCK

Spago is the sexy, fine-dining restaurant inside the Marina Bay Sands hotel (yea, it's that fancy). Spago does California cuisine (think crispy Sea Bass and juicy steak) with worldly influence and artistic plating.

Dinner here is a comprehensive experience with dishes and cocktails that keep you on your toes.

Open: 12 - 2:30 pm daily, 6 - 10 pm Sun- Thu, 6 - 11 pm Fr-Sat

Address: 1 Bayfront Ave, Tower 2

How to Get Up: Take the elevator in Tower 2 to level 55, then take the next lift to level 57.

CE LA VIE

This is one of the most iconic places to eat in Singapore – as it's also at the top of Marina Bay Sands! Ce La Vie is a bucket-list restaurant due, largely, to the view. It sits right next to the infinity pool overlooking the bay. While it offers stunning views, I've got to be honest – the food is just okay. My pro tip? Come for cocktails and an appetizer then move on to another fab restaurant on this list.

⊙ **Open:** 12 - 2:45 pm, 6 - 10:30 pm

⊕ **Address**: 1 Bayfront Ave, Tower 3

CUT BY WOLFGANG PUCK

Red wine and steak, anyone? CUT is known for the highest-quality cuts of meat and seafood in Singapore, as well as over 500 wines. Beautiful plating and top-notch service make this my vote for your special occasion dinners in Singapore.

⊙ **Open:** 5:30 - 10 pm Sun-Th, 5:30 - 11pm Fri-Sat

⊕ **Address**: The Shoppes at Marina Bay, 2 Bayfront Avenue

JAAN BY KIRK WESTAWAY

British cuisine is often overlooked in Singapore's luxury dining sphere… and most of the world's dining sphere, if were being honest. But JAAN by Kirk Westaway has certainly British food back on the culinary map with his Top-50 restaurant in Asia. JAAN focuses on sourcing English, Scottish, and Welsh ingredients to create buzz-worthy dishes worth every penny.

⊙ **Open:** 11:45 am - 1 pm, 6:30 - 8 pm. Closed Sunday.

⊕ **Address**: 2 Stamford Road, Swissotel

LANTERN ROOFTOP BAR

Lantern Rooftop Bar sits at the top of the Fullerton Bay Hotel and offers one of the best views of Marina Bay and Marina Bay Sands. They have a wide variety of wines, champagnes, and cocktails to sip on, plus mouthwatering tapas. THIS is date night.

⊙ **Open:** 10 - 1 am Sun-Th, 10 - 2 am Fr-Sat (cocktails from 3 pm onwards)

⊕ **Address**: 80 Collyer Quay

LAVO

If you're craving Italian-American, this is the place to go - located at the top of Marina Bay Sands, in the SkyPark. LAVO is particularly lively on Fridays and Saturdays, when the lounge turns into a nightclub.

🕒 **Open:** 10:30 - 1 am Sun-Th, 10:30 - 3 am Fr, 10:30 - 4 am Sat

🌐 **Address**: 10 Bayfront Ave, Tower 1

POLLEN

Located inside the Flower Dome in Gardens by the Bay, expect delicate afternoon tea, vegan plant-based set menus, and fragrant cocktails amongst a floral décor, underneath a glass rooftop with a botanical view. Bonus: You get free entry to the Flower Dome after dining at POLLEN.

🕒 **Open:** 12 - 2:30 pm, 6 - 9:30 pm, Closed Tuesdays

🌐 **Address**: Flower Dome, Gardens by the Bay, 18 Marina Gardens Drive

KINKI

Kinki is known for having fresh Japanese food and Japanese-inspired drinks. The restaurant is modern and grungy – in the most charming way – with a rooftop view of the Bay and of the Marina Bay Sands.

🕒 **Open:** 12:30 – 3 pm, 6 – 11 pm, Closed Sunday

🌐 **Address**: Customs House, 70 Collyer Quay

WHAT TO DO IN MARINA BAY

GARDENS BY THE BAY

The Supertrees of Gardens by the Bay have become one of Singapore's most iconic sights. Skyscraper trees with colorful neon branches makes you feel as if you've entered Avatar! Walking around the gardens is free, but there are also two domes, the Flower Dome and Cloud Forest, that you can pay to explore further (worth it). The Flower Dome is the home to a huge variety of plants and flowers, and the Cloud Forest has a tall indoor waterfall and replicates being amongst mystical mountains. This is a must!

Ticket cost: Free to walk around, $28 SGD for The Flower Dome and Cloud Forest

MARINA BAY LIGHT SHOW

Every night at 8 and 9 pm, with an additional 10 pm show on Fridays and Saturdays, there is a light and water show at the base of the Marina Bay Sands. Water geysers, lasers, and music all come together to create a beautiful show with the background of Marina Bay! Grab a seat in front of the Shoppes at Marina Bay for the best view!

Cost: Free!

Gardens by the Bay

F1

The Singapore Grand Prix is part of the Formula 1 (F1) circuit. While the main event is the motor race, tons of people go for the concerts and liveliness that F1 brings to the city. This race happens in September every year. If you're keen to see F1, book your tickets super early - the earliest ticket sales are usually in December the year before!

Ticket cost: starts at around $270 SGD and goes up to the high thousands.

ART SCIENCE MUSEUM

You have probably seen this museum somewhere on Instagram. FutureWorld is the permanent exhibit with an infinite amount of lights suspended from the ceiling that look like stars in the Milky Way. While the permanent exhibit is fabulous, the museum also has tons of incredible rotating exhibits. I highly recommend quickly googling the current exhibits, and if one seems interesting, tacking that onto your visit to the permanent collection.

Entry Fee: $18 for one exhibit, $30 for two exhibits

Hours: 10 am - 7 pm

☞ PRO TIP
Book these tickets ahead of time to get a time slot that works for you!

SINGAPORE FLYER

How are you with heights? Singapore Flyer is the highest Ferris wheel in all of Asia, giving amazing aerial views of the city, Marina Bay, the Singapore River, and Gardens by the Bay. It takes about thirty minutes to do one rotation – so worth the spend!

Ticket Cost: $33 (book online for a slight discount!)

Hours: 8:30 am - 10:30 pm

Singapore Flyer

WHERE TO SHOP IN MARINA BAY

THE SHOPPES AT MARINA BAY

This is how Singapore does malls. Inside The Shoppes at Marina Bay, you'll find a canal with gondolas, a huge fountain, and of course, all the luxury brands you can think of! There are also plenty of celebrity chef restaurants, a theatre, and a casino. There are 'regular' high street shops, as well, plus a food court if you get hungry.

Hours: 10:30 am - 11 pm

SUNTEC CITY

Need a new charger? Forget your sunglasses on the plane? Want some candy to bring home to your nephews? Suntec City is that random mall that sells it all. It's further from Marina Bay, towards the Central Business District – but it's huge! It was designed with feng shui in mind and so, has four different shopping zones, each specializing in gadgets, clothes, and/or souvenirs of some sort.

Hours: 10 am - 10 pm

LOUIS VUITTON

Okay okay, even if you're night buying a $15k purse, this Louis Vuitton, in particular, is a unique window-shopping experience. Floating right in the middle of the bay is Louis Vuitton island. You can either access it from outside the Shoppes at Marina Bay, though my favorite thing to do is to walk into the Louis Vuitton store inside the Shoppes at Marina Bay, then take the underground tunnel to the part of the store that's floating in the bay. The tunnel has the history of Louis Vuitton displayed and is quite interesting!

Hours: 10:30 am - 11:30 pm

CHAPTER TWO

Chinatown

WHERE OLD AND NEW MEET...PLUS, FOOD.

Buddhist temples next to Hindu Temples, murals painted by local artists, street stalls selling bright red lanterns and jade jewelry - Chinatown is a kaleidoscope of color in Singapore. In Chinatown, you'll be introduced to Singapore's past, with decades-old shophouses and beautiful temples still lining the streets. The area, however, is also keeping up with Singapore's fast pace of modernization, demonstrated by the numerous amounts of contemporary bars and restaurants.

This, my friends, is my favorite neighborhood in Singapore.

STREETS TO EXPLORE IN CHINATOWN

Exploring Chinatown is a whirlwind adventure! On one hand, you have the alleys in central Chinatown with all of the Buddhist trinkets, exotic souvenirs and temples galore. On the other, just outside of central Chinatown, you have a network of incredible streets with boutique shops, yoga studios, and fine dining spots just waiting to be discovered!

Here are a couple areas to start your Chinatown escapade.

PAGODA STREET

Pagoda Street is right in the center of Chinatown. You'll find hundreds of stalls lining the street side, selling affordable Singapore souvenirs as well as traditional Chinese goods. Wander down some of the alleys and you'll find you'll be able to buy traditional Chinese medicine (i.e. fungus, roots, and birds nest in jars), wax seal blocks or stamps with your name in Chinese characters. Even if you're not looking to buy anything, a stroll down Pagoda street is wonderful to immerse yourself into the liveliness of Chinatown culture.

KEONG SAIK ROAD

Keong Saik Road used to be Singapore's little Red-Light District, but now, is a trendy place to get drinks, go shopping in boutiques, and eat your heart out. It's definitely worth a wander, especially to take a look at the old traditional shophouses that line the street. Because Singapore is such a modern country, these little preserved pieces of history are a special reminder of what Singapore used to look like not too long ago. If you want to have a drink with a great view, visit Potato Head's rooftop.

ANN SIANG ROAD

Ann Siang Road is lined with shophouses but is also incredibly modern! On this street, you'll find so many cute cafes and restaurants, as well as trendy shops and upcoming designer pop-ups. There are also plenty of studio gyms where you can stop by for a yoga class or workout.

CLUB STREET

Club Street is best known for its weekends when the street comes alive with bars, clubs, and restaurants. During the day, it's a sleepy little street...but at night, it's where expats flock to blow off some steam. There are plenty of boutique stores and places to get Instagrammable meals and drinks! The shophouses here are in great condition, and it's a great street to wander around.

DUXTON HILL

Duxton Hill is one of my favorite areas to shop in Chinatown. It's similar to Ann Siang Road and Club Street but offers a slightly higher end vibe. The boutique stores are of better quality (and their prices reflect that), and quite a few famous chefs have opened hidden gem restaurants here. There are so many shops and eateries to be discovered on Duxton Hill.

• •

For more tips, articles, and packing guides—visit my blog at
▶ TheSoloGirlsTravelGuide.com

WHERE TO TO STAY IN CHINATOWN

♥ BUDGET

BEARY BEST! CHINATOWN

Here is the most affordable option in terms of dorms. This hostel isn't the fanciest or the prettiest – but it's clean, safe, and in a great location. And let me tell you an expert perk about this place – when dorm beds are open-concept (instead of closed pods), it is much easier to talk with your dorm mates and make friends. Don't let the retro lime green décor throw you off. I've stayed here and had a perfectly pleasant experience.

♥ **Style:** Dorms

💰 **Starts at:** $30 SGD

🌐 **Address:** 16 Upper Cross Street

Beary Best! Chinatown

TRIBE THEORY

This is an "Entrepreneurs Hostel for Startups and Digital Nomads" – in other words, a hostel for networking and meeting like-minded business-savvy travelers. This is genius! And best of all, this hostel isn't filled with people who are just looking to party and get wasted.

❤ **Style:** Dorms

💰 **Starts at:** $40 SGD

🌐 **Address::** 39 Ann Siang Rd, Chinatown, Singapore, Singapore, 069716

CUBE BOUTIQUE CAPSULE HOTEL

The cleanest, fanciest, and most comfortable hostel in all of Chinatown is right here! This is glamorous dorm living with pod capsules that feel like small hotel rooms complete with a reading light, electric socket and super comfy mattresses. Best of all, some dorm beds are equipped with a queen-sized mattress so that you can share with your bae. Breakfast is included!

❤ **Style:** dorms or privates

💰 **Starts at:** $65 SGD

🌐 **Address::** 76/78 Smith Street

❤ MID-RANGE

EIGHTEEN BY THREE CABINS

These aren't your typical capsule hotel rooms! Unlike the others, which are just a bed and some outlets, these capsule rooms have some space on the floor, allowing you to stand and stretch a little more. The communal spaces are full of tables, which is perfect for the girl who still needs to keep up with work in between activities. If you need a pick-me-up while working, there's a café right under the hotel.

❤ **Style:** Privates

💰 **Starts at:** $75 SGD

🌐 **Where:** on the border of Chinatown and the CBD

🌐 **Address::** 3 Stanley Street

HOTEL SOLOHA @ CHINATOWN

Stay here if you want to seriously up your Instagram game. This eclectic hotel is right next to Potato Head, one of the most photographed places in the area, and the fun continues inside the hotel. The reception doubles as a trendy bar, and the morning breakfast room transforms into a ramen bar in the evening. This hotel is ahead of aaalllll the trends. Plus, free drinks and coffee?! Yes please.

❤ **Style:** Privates

💰 **Starts at:** $120 SGD

🌐 **Where:** The heart of Chinatown

🌐 **Address:** 12-16 Teck Lim Road

ST SIGNATURE TANJONG PAGAR

This hotel makes arriving in Singapore a DREAM. After a long-haul flight, the last thing you want to do is make small talk as you check into your room, and this hotel's automated online check-in makes it super easy to get into your room stress-free. This Co-Living hotel is somewhere in between a boutique hotel and a hostel, with cozy private rooms and shared bathrooms and common areas. The best part? You're staying in a shophouse right above Chinatown's main street, so you're right in the center of the action.

❤ **Style:** Privates

💰 **Starts at:** $76 SGD

🌐 **Where:** The heart of Chinatown

🌐 **Address::** 273A South Bridge Road

HOTEL 1888 COLLECTION

This modern hotel is the for the girl who likes to completely unwind after a day of exploring – with cozy nights in all the snacks and tea. Each room is fitted with a projector screen – instant movie night! Plus, a kettle, a fridge, and all of Chinatown's food options within a few minutes' walk.

❤ **Style:** Privates

💰 **Starts at:** $74 SGD

🌐 **Where:** The heart of Chinatown

🌐 **Address:** 20 Trengganu Street

DORSETT SINGAPORE

Spacious! Finally! Forget the tiny hole-in-the-wall rooms that barely fit your luggage. The Dorsett has livable rooms that are a joy to come back to and collapse after an afternoon of adventuring! They've got a beautiful outdoor pool and the option to upgrade to a 2-story loft room! All of this, plus a great location, near Outram park MRT, which connects you to the East-West and North-East MRT lines!

♥ **Style:** Privates

💰 **Starts at:** $114 SGD

🌐 **Where:** near Outram Park MRT

🌐 **Address:** 333 New Bridge Rd

♥ LUXURY

AMOY HOTEL

This boutique hotel mixes Asian influence with modern decor. The hotel grounds feel like you're stepping into an old Chinese palace, with amazing art and architecture surrounding you. With all of the history on display, it feels like you're staying in a museum! Better yet, free airport transfers are included, so you can step off the plane and straight into the heart of Singapore without worrying about logistics.

♥ **Style:** Privates

💰 **Starts at:** $167 SGD

🌐 **Where:** In between Chinatown and Marina Bay

🌐 **Address:** 76 Telok Ayer St

ANN SIANG HOUSE

The Ann Siang House tailors your room to your style of travel. Choose a standard, modern rooms – or specialty rooms like The Culinary Studio with a fully fitted kitchen (plus some pasta essentials), the Wellbeing Suite with a massage chair, essential oils and large bathtub (& bath salts!) or the Active Studio, with an in-room stationary bike, weights, yoga mat, and medicine ball.

♥ **Style:** Privates

💰 **Starts at:** $260 SGD

🌐 **Where:** The heart of Chinatown

🌐 **Address:** 28 Ann Siang Road

KESA HOUSE

A hotel set inside an iconic shophouse of Singapore. This hotel is on Keong Saik Road, known for being one of the most picturesque streets in the city. Some rooms have terraces, and all have access to a shared kitchen! But you will probably be eating out anyways as KeSa House is walking distance to tons of restaurants including Singapore's famous Michelin restaurant (Liao Fan Hong Kong Soya Sauce Chicken Rice & Noodles) on the same street.

♥ **Style:** Privates

💰 **Starts at:** $191 SGD

🌐 **Where:** In between Outram Park and Chinatown

🌐 **Address:** 55 Keong Saik Road

SIX SENSES MAXWELL

Asian influence with a European twist – Six Senses Maxwell is a beautiful hotel to spend a few days. Just slightly further outside the crowded streets of Chinatown, you are guaranteed a quiet night's sleep. Then wake up for brunch at the Cook & Tras Social Library and come back for cocktails and spirits at Garcha's and Rose Lounge & Bar. There's also a gym, rooftop pool, and best of all – is walking distance to Maxwell Food Center.

♥ **Style:** Privates

💰 **Starts at:** $205 SGD

🌐 **Where:** Towards Tanjong Pagar

🌐 **Address:** 2 Cook Street

SIX SENSES DUXTON

Want a glamourous yet intimate hotel stay in Singapore? Forget big chain hotels; Six Senses Duxton is all about elegant architecture, thought-provoking artwork, sexy lighting, and intriguing menus for both cocktails and dinner. Located in a 19th Century shophouse, the opulent vintage décor brings Singapore's history to life.

♥ **Style:** Privates

💰 **Starts at:** $300 SGD

🌐 **Where:** Tanjong Pagar, close to Chinatown

🌐 **Address:** 83 Duxton Road

☞ **FUN FACT**

You'll hear a lot of "Singlish" spoken in Singapore (Singaporean-English). Example: Simply saying "can"/"cannot" are other ways of saying yes and no. You'll also probably hear 'lah' at the end of sentences. This is just a friendly way to end a sentence.

WHERE TO EAT IN CHINATOWN

Chinatown is home to some of the best hawker centers in Singapore! And these hawker centers are a great place to eat when you're on a budget...but they're also my 1st choice to eat even if I've got pockets stuffed full of cash!

♥ BUDGET EATS

CHINATOWN COMPLEX

Come hungry. This complex is HUGE, with hundreds of stalls! Everyone here has perfected their signature dish, so you really can't go wrong. There's even a stall for craft beers! This place can get busy during peak hours, but in my opinion, that's half the fun! Don't miss Liao Fan Hong Kong Soya Sauce Chicken Rice & Noodle Stall, located inside this complex; it's the cheapest Michelin-star meal in the world!

Open: 7 am -10 pm daily

Address: 335 Smith Street

MAXWELL HAWKER CENTER

My favorite hawker center in Singapore - known for having the best chicken rice in all the land! Tian Tian Hainanese Chicken Rice is where you'll find the famous Chicken Rice dish (duh), but Zhen Zhen Porridge and Shanghai Tim-Sum are also incredibly highly-regarded with it comes to Chicken Rice. Why not try both and compare?

Open: 8 am - 2 am daily

Address: 1 Kadayanallur St

Maxwell Hawker Centre by ImipolexG

CHINATOWN FOOD STREET

Chinatown Food Street is one of the more famous places to hunt for food. You can stroll down the street, passing by food stalls and stopping when one catches your eye. Honest moment: I enjoy the overall experience of strolling a food street and spontaneously choosing a dish. It must be done! But, I personally, prefer hawker centers when it comes to authenticity.

◉ **Open:** 11 am - 11 pm

⊕ **Address:** Smith Street, Singapore

TIONG BAHRU MARKET

The #1 place to get a hawker breakfast in Singapore. There's a wet market on the bottom floor, with the hawker center on the second floor. You can get everything from rice porridge to dim sum to noodle dishes for breakfast. I highly recommend either the rice porridge or kaya toast! Pro Tip: Find some deep-fried dough to dip on your coffee or milk tea!

◉ **Open:** 9 am - 8 pm, though the first breakfast stalls open at 7 am and close before noon.

⊕ **Address:** 30 Seng Poh Road

TONG HENG CONFECTIONERY

Also known as Tong Heng Delicacies, this bakery is full of delectable buttery pastries. I highly recommend the egg tart, the coconut egg tart, and the pork bun. These pastries melt in your mouth and are only about $2 SGD each. A must try!

◉ **Open:** 9 am - 9 pm daily

⊕ **Address:** 285 South Bridge Road

♥ MID-RANGE EATS

HIAO YA TOU

Xiao Ya Tou can be roughly translated to 'Little Rebel' in Chinese. This incredible restaurant takes classic Singaporean dishes and elevates them to gourmet levels. Try the XYT Dumplings with black vinegar chili oil or the Slow-Cooked Pork Rendang for a taste of Singapore – with a twist. Psst: Vegetarian options available.

Open: 12-11 pm M-Th, 12 pm - 12 am Fr, 10 am - 12 am Sat, 10 am - 5pm Sun

Address: 6 Duxton Hill

YUM CHA

Eat like a local at Yum Cha - a bit of a hidden gem in Chinatown. It's a little hard to find, located on the second floor on a side street of Temple Street (follow Google Maps). Once you walk up the inconspicuous stairs, you're greeted with a lively, loud dim sum house. The food arrives in the traditional bamboo baskets -best for sharing!

Open: 10:30 am - 10:30 pm on weekdays, 9 am - 10:30 pm on weekends

Address: 20 Trengganu Street, off of Temple St

CHINATOWN SEAFOOD RESTAURANT

Clever name, huh? At least you know what you're getting at this outdoor seafood spot with super casual vibes and super yummy dishes (especially their chili crab). It has a similar lively atmosphere to that of a hawker center, but as an actual restaurant – you don't have to hustle to find an available table!

Open: 12-12:30 pm

Address: 51 Pagoda Street

♥ LUXURY EATS

TIPPLING CLUB

The Tippling Club is known for two things: their extensive cocktail menu and their tasting menu. Their house cocktails are creative and inspired by both history and food, and their tasting menus are either 5 or 12 courses. They'll set you back a couple hundred dollars, but if you want a meal/foodie experience you'll never forget, this is it!

◔ **Open:** 12 pm - 12 am, closed Sunday

⊕ **Address:** 38 Tanjong Pagar Road

ESQUINA

Esquina is a modern Spanish restaurant in the heart of Chinatown. They aim to take you to Spain with the flavors of their food and the atmosphere of the restaurant. They have the option of a tasting menu, or you can choose to dine a la carte. Oh, and if they've got the Lobster Paella available – don't hesitate.

◔ **Open:** 12-2:30 pm, 6-10:30 pm Tues - Sat. Closed Sunday and Monday.

⊕ **Address:** 16 Jiak Chuan Road

BURNT ENDS

Burnt Ends has one simple rule: everything on their menu must touch their signature oven. The menu changes each day, which means you'll never get bored of returning. Burnt Ends has made a name for itself by grabbing a spot on the list of Asia's Top 50 restaurants.

◔ **Open:** 6 pm - 12 am Tu-Th, 11:45 am - 2 pm & 6 pm - 12 am on weekends.
Closed Mon & Tues.

⊕ **Address:** 20 Teck Lim Road

WHAT TO DO IN CHINATOWN

Chinatown is the cultural hub of Singapore. This neighborhood reflects all of the incredible cultures that come together to create the collective identity of Singapore. When in Chinatown, learn a little more about each of the unique places that have shaped Singapore to be such a vibrant melting pot.

FREE WALKING TOUR

Soak up the culture and history of Chinatown in one morning via a delightful stroll with your English-speaking tour guide. You'll walk through the most iconic streets and historical spots where you'll learn facts and tidbits about Singapore that you'd never absorb on your own. And while this is Chinatown, you'll be introduced to both Buddhist and Hindu temples.

Contact: There are two companies to check out for free walking tours: Indie Singapore and Monster Day Tours.

Ps. Both of these companies offer free walking tours in other parts of the island that are equally fascinating.

Pss. Many temples I mention below are included in this 3-hour tour!

How Much: Totally free – but customary to tip whatever you feel ($10-$20 is my suggestion).

CHINATOWN HERITAGE CENTER

Did you that Singapore is a country largely built off the backs of Chinese immigrants? The Chinatown Heritage Center has preserved and restore 3 shophouses which show you what a typical shophouse would have looked like in the 1950s – including the dorms which housed these immigrant workers in wildly-cramped conditions. Come with curiosity and walk away with a new level of respect for this intricate culture.

Ticket Cost: $18 with multimedia guide, $25 for a guided tour

English Tour Times: 11:30 am, 1:30 pm, 4:30 pm

🌐 **Address:** 48 Pagoda Street

🕐 **Hours:** 9:30 am - 6:30 pm daily

SRI MARIAMMAN TEMPLE

Come learn a little about Hinduism. This Dravidian-style Hindu temple is the oldest in Singapore. Its colorful entryway is stunning and it's truly an important part of Singapore's history. It was constructed in 1827 by an Indian pioneer and it was the only place to register Hindu marriages at the time.

Entry Cost: Free, but if you're taking photos a small donation is requested

🕐 **Hours:** 7 am - 12 pm, 6-9 pm daily

Sri Mariamman Temple

NUS BABA HOUSE

The NUS Baba House is an amazing shophouse restored by the National University of Singapore. It shows what a traditional Peranakan shophouse looked like, as well as some art pieces that further demonstrate Peranakan culture. Peranakan Culture is an important aspect of Singapore – it's the result of culturally rich ethnicities melting together, with touches of Portuguese and Dutch influences.

> ☞ **PRO TIP**
>
> This museum is by-appointment only and appointments usually fill up pretty quickly. Book ahead if this is something you'd like to see. You can book from the 15th of every month, two months ahead. English guided tours are Tues-Fri at 10 am, and self-guided visits are on Saturdays at 1:30, 2:15, 3:15, and 4 pm.

Entry Fee: $10

⊕ **Address:** 157 Neil Road

THIAN HOCK KENG TEMPLE

This temple is very important to the Hokkien Chinese of Singapore. The temple celebrates the Goddess of the Sea, Mazu, and is Singapore's oldest Buddhist temple. It used to be located on the waterfront, but as Singapore has expanded, it's has moved closer inland (the temple didn't move, Singapore just built over the sea). Incredibly ornate and built in the Southern Chinese architectural style, this temple shouldn't be missed!

Entry Fee: free!

⊙ **Hours:** 7:30 am - 5:30 pm

> ☞ **FUN FACT**
>
> Singaporeans are the fastest pedestrians! Make sure you walk quickly!

CHAPTER THREE

Kampong Glam
THE HIPSTER HOOD

Kampong Glam is the amazing gem of a neighborhood that, somehow, so many travelers miss out on! Here you can find artsy streets and funky shops with cute cafes mixed in-between! The must-see spots? Haji Lane – a street splashed with paint and murals - and Arab Street with middle eastern restaurants and shisha spots!

WHERE TO STAY IN KAMPONG GLAM

Accommodation in the Kampong Glam and Bugis area is catered more-so to the budget and mid-range traveler. This is the area where you'll find affordable accommodation and eats, yes - but this area is still definitely worth visiting even if you're a strictly-luxury traveler.

♥ BUDGET

BEARY BEST! HOSTEL @ KAMPONG GLAM

My #1 choice of hostel in Kampong Glam is easily Beary Best! Hostel. The dorms are top-notch; the designers have really thought of everything to elevate dorm living into a glamorous experience. You have a pod bed (like a cubby in the wall) with a reading light, outlet, and little wall pocket to keep organized. What I love most is the rooftop area, good for drinking a 7-Eleven beer while people watching Arab Street below. #BestLocationEver.

♥ **Style:** Dorms

💰 **Starts at:** $37 SGD / $27 USD

🌐 **Where:** Next to Arab Street

🌐 **Address:** 64 Arab street

CUBE BOUTIQUE CAPSULE HOTEL @ KAMPONG GLAM

Female dorms, small rooms with 3 beds, twin beds, queen beds…you've got all the options at this chic capsule hostel. Travel solo and feel safe with just women sleeping nearby, or travel with your girlfriends and get a room together – while still having the option to be social in the common spaces where other travelers hang. Ps. Free breakfast and who doesn't love that?

♥ **Style:** Privates

💰 **Starts at:** $55 SGD/$40 USD

🌐 **Where:** Near Arab Street

🌐 **Address:** 55 Bussorah St

MET A SPACE POD @ ARAB STREET

Futuristic as fuck. Sleep in a space pod where you can shut your pod door and get some serious ME-TIME with your own flat screen TV inside your pod. Plus, each unit has it's own air conditioning, so you can regulate the temperature of your capsule. While you share a bathroom and common area, this kind of accommodation gives you a lot of privacy and it feels less like a hostel and more like a very small hotel. Staying here is a bucket-list item for sure.

♥ **Style:** In between dorms and private

💰 **Starts at:** $60 SGD / $44 USD

🌐 **Where:** On Arab Street!

🌐 **Address:** 56 Arab Street

♥ MID-RANGE

ZEN PREMIUM KAMPONG GLAM

An affordable mid-spend that is only slightly higher priced than a fancy dorm room round' here. When you just want to be alone in a clean, safe hotel room with a few perks (like a breezy terrace for reading a book or a little café where you can grab a coffee and work) – without breaking the bank, this is it. I vote this as my #1 layover hotel.

♥ **Style:** Privates

💰 **Starts at:** $78 SGD / $85 USD

🌐 **Where:** The heart of Kampong Glam

🌐 **Address:** 101 Jln Sultan

HOTEL BOSS

Cozy rooms perfectly sized for a solo traveler! Stay here for the perks which include a view over the Sultan Mosque, complimentary Asian-style breakfast, restaurants within the hotel, and a gym that overlooks the rooftop pool. I mean, is there a better way to cool off after your workout than jumping in the water? Located right next to Victoria Street, there are also plenty of places to grab food or make a friend or two.

💰 **Starts at:** $108 SGD / $80 USD

🌐 **Where:** Outskirts of Kampong Glam

🌐 **Address:** 500 Jalan Sultan

DESTINATION SINGAPORE BEACH ROAD

Swanky! Let's talk about the rooftop pool overlooking the city! Or the glitzy hotel bar and restaurant where you can casually hang out wearing red lipstick and maybe catch the eye of a cute traveler. But that's just me and my vibe...don't judge. Noone cute in the hotel? No worries, there are plenty of bars and restaurants right outside the door where you can go get social!

♥ **Style:** Privates

💰 **Starts at:** $120 SGD / $87 USD

🌐 **Where:** Near the water that connects to Marina Bay

🌐 **Address:** 700 Beach Road

THE SULTAN

Absolute perfection. Honestly, you can just stop searching for your hotel here. This beautiful boutique hotel is represents comfort, style, and service perfectly. The staff go above and beyond to take care of you – as this is a small hotel, you won't go unnoticed. The breakfast is lovely, the shophouse setting is charming and the location makes for a great base to explore Kampong Glam.

♥ **Style:** Privates

💰 **Starts at:** $131 SGD / $96 USD

🌐 **Where:** Central Kampong Glam

🌐 **Address:** 101 Jalan Sultan

The Sultan

♥ LUXURY

INTERCONTINENTAL SINGAPORE

The fanciest hotel in the area, The Intercontinental Singapore is located right in the heart of Bugis, next to Kampong Glam. The pool sits above the busy streets of Bugis and it's the best place to get some sun. The hotel is located right in Bugis Junction, a busy shopping mall, but still manages to be an oasis away from the bustle below. The breakfast buffet is also a big plus, with fresh smoothies, pastries, and everything else you could want!

♥ **Style:** Privates

💰 **Starts at:** $200 SGD

🌐 **Where:** Bugis, outside of Kampong Glam

🌐 **Address:** 80 Middle Road

> **NOTE**
> Kampong Glam doesn't have any super luxurious places to stay, as it's known for being more of a trendy, underground area. However - Bugis, just next to Kampong Glam, has the Intercontinental, a really beautiful hotel, that's just a short walk away from Kampong Glam.

WHERE TO EAT IN KAMPONG GLAM

♥ BUDGET EATS

Budget food options in Kampong Glam are plentiful and often some of the more delicious places to eat. You can't go wrong with a kebab from the corner shop if you need something quick, but if you have a little more time and want to try some local food, the Indonesian and Muslim Singaporean food in Kampong Glam is the best! Here are some of my favorite places.

ZAM ZAM

Zam Zam is loved throughout Singapore for their murtabak. Murtabak is dough stuffed with meats and other vegetables or eggs. Zam Zam makes all sorts of amazing Indian-Muslim food. The Roti Pratha is a great savory breakfast option - it's a pan-fried dough, traditionally served with a curry. Absolutely the best way to start the day.

⊙ **Open:** 7 am - 11 pm

⊕ **Address:** 699 North Bridge Road

HJH MAIMUNAH RESTAURANT

This restaurant is known for their Nasi Padang. Nasi Padang is steamed rice with a bunch of different choices of Indonesian curries and vegetables. Hjh Maimunah Restaurant has one of the best in Singapore to offer Nasi Padang! Order a few bites to stay cheap – or fill up a giant plate of food for $10 Singapore dollars.

⊙ **Open:** 7 am - 8 pm, closed Sundays

⊕ **Address:** 11 Jalan Pisang

RUMAH MAKAN MINANG

This is another restaurant that is well-loved for their Nasi Padang. The way it works? Choose from a selection of buffet-style treats, picking and choosing what goes on your plate as you go. The most popular choice here is the beef rendang!

🕐 **Open:** 8:30 am - 7:30 pm daily

🌐 **Address:** 18 Kandahar Street

KAMPONG GLAM CAFE

Kampong Glam Cafe serves affordable and authentic Malay food. My favorite dishes here are the Soto Ayam (chicken soup with rice noodles) and the Nasi Lemak (coconut rice with peanuts, little fish, and usually another protein). The teh tarik (pulled tea) is milky, sweet, and a must when coming here.

🕐 **Open:** 8 am - 2 am, closed Mondays

🌐 **Address:** 17 Bussorah Street

NOODLE THAI THAI KITCHEN

Ask anyone in Kampong Glam for a food recommendation and odds are that they'll point you towards Noodle Thai Thai Kitchen. Dishes run from about $4-10 Singapore dollars. Unlike a lot of other budget options in Singapore, this is a restaurant and not a food stall, so it's great if you want to take a break from Hawker centers and treat yourself to a nice sit-down Thai meal.

🕐 **Open:** 11:30 am - 3 pm, 5-11pm weekdays, 12-11 pm weekends

🌐 **Address:** 327 Beach Road

♥ MID-RANGE EATS

The mid-ranged restaurants in Kampong Glam are usually where the 'trendy' side of Singapore can be seen. Influence from around the world comes together with Kampong Glam's middle eastern and Indonesian roots, and the mid-ranged restaurants reflect the melting pot that Kampong Glam is today!

ALATURKA

Alaturka is one of the most well-known restaurants in Kampong Glam. This Mediterranean and Turkish restaurant has tiled decor that transports you straight out of Singapore and into Turkey. The food comes in pretty large portions and is really flavorful so bring your appetite.

◉ **Open:** 12-11 pm Sun - Thu, 12-11:30 pm Fri & Sat

⊕ **Address:** 15 Bussorah Street

FIKA SWEDISH CAFE & BISTRO

Fika was started by a Swedish & Singaporean couple who brought the flavors of Scandinavia to Asia. They are a health-minded café, using seasonal ingredients to bring you a meal to sooth your stomach, mind, body, and soul. After a week of fried food, here is where you can look forward to fresh salads and wellness bowls!

◉ **Open:** 11 am - 10 pm Sun-Thur, 11 am - 11 pm Friday, 11:30 am - 11 pm Sat

⊕ **Address:** 257 Beach Road

PITA BAKERY

Pita Bakery is one of the best vegan and vegetarian options in Singapore. They make some of the best pita in Singapore and have plenty of dips like hummus and babaganoush. The falafel are also really popular here – it'd be a crime not to try em'.

◉ **Open:** 10 am - 8:30 pm Mon-Thurs, 10 am - 9:30 pm Fri-Sat, 9 am - 9:30 pm Sun

⊕ **Address:** 29 Bali Lane

THE BEAST SOUTHERN KITCHEN + BOURBON BAR

If you're getting sick of Asian food and need a taste of the Southern US, you need to come here! This is the only place in Singapore you can find cornbread! AND they have an impressive collection of bourbon in-house, including barrels full of homemade bourbon, to make their creative bourbon cocktails.

Open: 5 pm - 12 am Mon-Wed, 5 pm - 1 am Thurs & Fri, 11 - 12 am on weekends

Address: 17 Jalan Klapa

SELFIE COFFEE

Selfie Coffee is an incredibly fun place to have an iced coffee. You order your iced drink, take a selfie on their in-house phone, and wait. Your coffee will have foam with your selfie printed out on it! The coffees are pricier than a regular coffee, but the experience, and getting to drink your face, is totally worth it for the Gram. That's right...take a selfie with your selfie.

Open: 10 am - 7 pm Mon-Thu, 10 am - 9 pm Fri-Sun

Address: 11 Haji Lane

FLYING MONKEY

Flying Monkey has a great atmosphere and Indian tapas. This is a great option for solo travelers because you get to try a bunch of different dishes without having to box up leftovers. It's a very lively restaurant, especially on weekends and evenings, when people come for the Indian-inspired cocktails.

Open: 12 - 2:30 pm, 5:30 - 11 pm. Open until 11:55 on Friday and Saturday and closed on Monday.

Address: 67 Bussorah Street

☞ FUN FACT

Ever heard of the fruit called Durian? Durian is an incredibly smelly fruit. So smelly they're banned in shopping malls and on public transportation - you could be fined for carrying one inside!

For more tips, articles, and packing guides—visit my blog at
▶ TheSoloGirlsTravelGuide.com

♥ LUXURY EATS

NOX DINE IN THE DARK

At NOX, you're signing up for a fine-dining experience in total darkness. The point? To lose yourself in the taste, texture and fragrance of every dish. All of the staff is blind or visually-impaired, guiding you through your four-course meal for an unforgettable food journey.

Open: 6-10 pm

Address: 269 Beach Road

SCALED BY AH HUA KELONG

Scaled by Ah Hua Kelong uses locally caught and farmed fish (never importing fish or seafood from abroad) to create a beautiful seafood-focused menu. All of the fish is caught that day, making it an incredibly fresh meal with an emphasis on farm-to-table eating. Pro Tip: Try the Chili Crab Risotto.

Open: 5:30-10:30 pm, closed Mondays

Address: 55 Haji Lane

POSITANO RISTO

This is a halal restaurant that locals love for authentic Italian dishes. The lobster risotto and soft-shell crab are some of their most popular dishes, though you can't go wrong with a classic pasta or pizza.

Open: 11:30 am - 9:30 pm Sun-Thur, 11:30 am - 10:30 pm Fri & Sat

Address: 66 Bussorah St

☞ **PRO TIP**

Make reservations for these bad boys.

WHAT TO DO IN KAMPONG GLAM

Bougie on a budget. Dress up, stroll the trendy streets, window shop, stop for a crafted coffee...and repeat. I love Kampong Glam.

HAJI LANE

Haji Lane is a must-visit in Kampong Glam. The small street is lined with trendy restaurants and bars, as well as sweet cafes and unique boutiques. There are incredible and colorful murals lining the street, as well. This is definitely one of the cutest streets in Singapore, as well as one of the most Instagrammable!

Cost: Free!

◉ **Hours:** 24/7 but most alive during the from noon to midnight!

ARAB STREET

Arab Street is in the heart of Kampong Glam! Here you'll find middle eastern shops where you can buy intricate lamps and gorgeous carpets, as well as wall tiles and glass jewelry. If you like to sew or craft, there are so many shops that sell unique fabrics and ribbons for all your crafty and creative projects.

Cost: Free

◔ **Hours:** Most stores are open from 10 am to 6 pm.

BUSSORAH STREET

Hungry? Here's your foodie street. There are plenty of restaurants lining the street – and plenty of handsome bar men trying to entice you to sit down. But even if you aren't hungry, come and sit down for the people watching alone. Order a Turkish tea and admire the view of Masjid Sultan - the most beautiful mosque in all of Kampong Glam!

Cost: Free!

◔ **Hours:** 24/7!

MASJID SULTAN

This is Singapore's most well-known mosque. It's located right in central Kampong Glam, and it's an absolutely stunning place of worship. Its gold dome can be seen from all over Kampong Glam, glittering in the afternoon sun. You can actually enter the mosque, but make sure you're wearing appropriate clothing. Women must wear long-sleeved shirts and bottoms that reach your ankles. You can also get an English tour when you visit to dive a bit deeper into the history and customs.

◔ **Visiting Hours:** 10 am - 12 pm, 2-4 pm Sat-Thurs, 2:30 - 4 pm Fridays

Cost: Free

⊕ **Address:** 3 Muscat Street

MASJID HAJJAH FATIMAH

This masjid, meaning 'mosque' in Malayu, was designed with both Islamic and European architectural styles. It's also a historical place in Singapore, completed in the mid-1800s, nearly 100 years before Singapore was a country! It's tower's foundation is on sand, which has led the mosque to having the nickname of "Singapore's Leaning Tower."

◷ **Hours:** 9 am - 9 pm

Cost: Free

⊕ **Address:** 4001 Beach Road

> ☞ **FUN FACT**
>
> Singapore is the only country to gain independence unwillingly - they were expelled from Malaysia!

• •

For more tips, articles, and packing guides—visit my blog at
▶ **TheSoloGirlsTravelGuide.com**

SHOPPING IN KAMPONG GLAM

ARAB STREET & HAJI LANE

I know I've already mentioned these streets, but damn, they're great AND serve multiple purposes. Arab Street and Haji Lane are my favorite adventure streets in Singapore as they're filled with artsy shops where you can find one-of-a-kind clothing, pottery, fabric, and gifts.

SUPERMAMA

This is what you get when you mix a craft store with an art gallery. Come to this store to look at all of the cute Singapore-themed art and end up leaving with a gift to take home to everyone in your family. Supermama has plates with iconic Singapore sights, stunning Peranakan dishware, Singaporean-recipe tea towels, and other practical, yet beautiful, Singapore souvenirs (that won't be shoved in a closet and forgotten forever...like most of the gifts I give to my family. #Ungrateful).

⊙ **Hours:** 11 am - 8 pm daily

⊕ **Address:** 265 Beach Road

BUGIS STREET MARKET

The Bugis Street Market is lively, buzzing with people, and full of cheap eats and trinkets. This is the closest thing you'll get to a typical Southeast-Asian market in Singapore- minus the haggling. The bottom floor is lined with food stalls (I recommend a fruit juice) and trendy knick knacks like selfie sticks and fidget spinners. Cute, but the floors above are where you really want to go. The top of the Bugis Street Market is a little bit of a hidden gem - most tourists don't know a top floor exists! This is where you'll find cheap clothes and shoes and purses - it's a maze of girly stalls!

⊙ **Hours:** 11 am - 10 pm

⊕ **Address:** New Bugis Street

BUGIS JUNCTION

Air-conditioning and snacks. Need I say more? Here is where the MRT is located with a little mall located inside a shophouse complex. This place represents a traditional mall in Asia with a couple shops you've heard of (Adidas and Aldo) and many you've never heard of. There are coffee stands, electronics stores and of course, a food court on the top floor. Even if you're not shopping, here is your chance to see how locals spend their weekends indoors and out of the heat.

- **Hours:** 10 am - 10 pm
- **Address:** 200 Victoria Street

> ☞ **FUN FACT**
> Singapore's crime rate is so low that some shops don't lock their doors or clear their market merchandise at night.

CHAPTER FOUR
Little India
FRESH MARKETS, COLORFUL FABRICS
AND INSANE FOOD!

Little India is a small neighborhood with a BIG personality. The people are friendly, the smells of spices float down the street, and there's food everywhere! Little India is also one of the best neighborhoods in Singapore for shopping. They've got markets galore!

72   LITTLE INDIA

However, Little India is often a neighborhood that people skip out on and overlook; it's just not on the tourist radar. That means that Indian culture remains pretty strong here without being watered down by tourist vibes.

All that being said…I've gotta say this: as a woman, Little India not the first place I'd recommend staying, Come to this neighborhood and prepared to be stared at as a western woman walking around Little India. You're fine. You're safe. But men just might be a little more excited/surprised to see you here than they would be in Chinatown or Kampong Glam. So, dress modestly. Don't accept invitations for tea. Don't walk alone at night.

But do come for a day-trip or if you're comfortable with all of the above, stay and enjoy.

> ☞ **FUN FACT**
>
> Singapore is one of three remaining city-states in the world, besides Monaco and the Vatican City.

For more tips, articles, and packing guides—visit my blog at
▶ **TheSoloGirlsTravelGuide.com**

WHERE TO STAY

♥ BUDGET

Little India is catered to the budget traveler. Yes, Kampong Glam also offers a big hostel scene but Kampong Glam is a little more upscale, whereas Little India has the cheapest hostel options if you're on a tight budget.

THE INNCROWD BACKPACKERS HOSTEL

This is by far the best traditional hostel in Singapore. There's a great atmosphere in this hostel, and they provide free breakfast and a Scooter tour. Like all traditional hostels in Singapore, this one is a bit outdated, but you've come here for the traveler experience, social vibes, and whacky budget adventures. Embrace it.

- ♥ **Style:** Dorms or privates
- 💰 **Starts at:** $18 SGD
- ⊕ **Where:** The heart of Little India, near Rocher MRT
- ⊕ **Address:** 73 Dunlop Street

FOOTPRINTS HOSTEL

Footprints Hostel is another traditional hostel in Singapore. It's one of the nicer hostels in Singapore, clean, with lockers and laundry. It's located in a great area and there's quick access to three different MRT stations nearby.

- ♥ **Style:** Dorms
- 💰 **Starts at:** $30 SGD
- ⊕ **Where:** The heart of Little India
- ⊕ **Address:** 25A Perak Road

7 WONDERS HOSTEL UPPER DICKSON

This is a nicer hostel in Singapore, with beds with curtains, providing more privacy than a traditional hostel. You get TWO pillows, linens, and a reading light in your bed, as well as access to a locker. There are two locations of the 7 Wonders Hostel, so make sure you're booking the Upper Dickson location! Oh, and they provide an airport shuttle for $9 per person! Savin' those dollas, girl!

- ♥ **Style:** Dorms
- 💰 **Starts at:** $28 SGD
- 🌐 **Where:** Near the Little India MRT
- 🌐 **Address:** 12A Upper Dickson Road

♥ MID-RANGE

HOLIDAY INN EXPRESS SERANGOON

Stay here if you want a great night's sleep after a full day of Singapore adventures! The beds are lush and the soundproofing in the rooms ensures you have a calm oasis to return to after visiting the hustle and bustle of Little India. This hotel is for the girl who likes winding down in her own space while still being in the center of Singapore's most vibrant neighborhood!

- ♥ **Style:** Privates
- 💰 **Starts at:** $149 SGD
- 🌐 **Where:** Outskirts of Little India
- 🌐 **Address:** 270 Jalan Basar

HILTON GARDEN INN SERANGOON

Let's just start with the outdoor pool. There are HUGE two person sunbeds, so you can spread out and seriously relax while workin' on your tan. In the evening, the pool view over Little India's shophouses with the CBD in the background is a prime sunset spot. And minimalist travelers, this hotel is for you – there are washing machines for use so you can stretch your wardrobe, an in-house shop in case you need a new toiletry or snack, and computers available in case you need to print out a boarding pass or two.

- ♥ **Style:** Privates
- 💰 **Starts at:** $152 SGD

⊕ **Where:** Heart of Little India

⊕ **Address:** 3 Belilios Road

CITADINES ROCHOR

This is a great place to stay if you want the comforts of home in Singapore. This modern apartment-hotel offers studios and suites with kitchenettes. It's right in the heart of Little India, so it's in a convenient location and surrounded by shopping and food.

♥ **Style:** Private apartments

💰 **Starts at:** $161 SGD

⊕ **Where:** Heart of Little India

⊕ **Address:** 2 Serangoon Road

♥ LUXURY

THE VAGABOND CLUB, SINGAPORE, A TRIBUTE PORTFOLIO HOTEL

This is a stunning hotel and is my top pick if you're looking for a glamorous and inviting place to stay. From the swanky, sexy bar where you'd DEFINITELY find the next James Bond to the velvety, sensual rooms, this hotel focuses on living with art, and you can certainly tell. And let's not forget about all the perks! Complimentary movies, a phone with data to explore with, free breakfast, AND access to the gym across the street? It doesn't get better.

♥ **Style:** Privates

💰 **Starts at:** $288 SGD

⊕ **Where:** In between Little India and Bugis, on the outskirts of both neighborhoods

⊕ **Address:** 39 Syed Alwi Road

ONE FARRER HOTEL

This hotel has everything! The main draws to this hotel are the large outdoor pool, the amazing jacuzzi (dreamy!), and the gym. You also have the option of staying in an apartment or classic hotel room, so you can choose the amount of space you need. And don't get me started on the breakfast – what other hotel has chefs making your food from scratch?!

♥ **Style:** Privates or apartments

💰 **Starts at:** $188 SGD

🌐 **Where:** Outskirts of Little India, near City Square Mall.

🌐 **Address:** 1 Farrer Park Station Road

For more tips, articles, and packing guides—visit my blog at
▶ **TheSoloGirlsTravelGuide.com**

WHERE TO EAT IN LITTLE INDIA

As authentic as you can get without actually flying to India, eating in Little India is unlike anything you've ever experienced. Most Indian food in Singapore's Little India is derived from the Southern Indian state of Tamil Nadu; with a few Northern Indian food spots scattered in-between.

In Little India, you'll find Indian food hawker centers with super-cheap (but still super authentic) Indian stalls, but you'll also find some lovely sit-down restaurants where you can order a whole spread.

♥ BUDGET EATS

TEKKA CENTER

The main hawker center in Little India – with a fresh market attached. Tekka Center makes for fun adventure. As you get off the MRT, you'll make your way through the market filled with spices and fresh fruit – coming out into the hawker station. Careful, though – not all food is created equal here. If you're standing in the center of the hawker center (you'll understand it when you see it) skip all the stalls surrounding, you. Go one row back. The most authentic stalls are positioned behind the front-and-center stalls.

⊙ **Open:** 6:30 am – 9pm pm

⊕ **Where:** Next to Little India MRT station

KOMALAS VILAS

This is by far my favorite place to eat in Little India. This vegetarian restaurant offers traditional Southern Indian food, specifically from Tamil

Nadu, and the food is absolutely delicious. I recommend the poori set, though you really can't go wrong!

Open: 7 am - 10:30 pm

Address: 76-78 Serangoon Road

MADRAS NEW WOODLANDS

This is the place to go if you want a full thali set. Thali sets are meals that come with rice or chapati, and often lentil and vegetable curries, though other curries are sometimes added. They're always amazing and every place that has a thali set will do it their own way - usually using family recipes!

Open: 7:30 am - 10:30 pm

Address: 14 Upper Dickson Road

JAGGI'S NORTHERN INDIAN CUISINE

Jaggi's is known for having great Northern Indian food. Most of Singapore's Indian population is Tamil, from the South. Jaggi's offers Northern food, which has a different taste. Most food here is Punjabi, but it's one of the few places you'll be able to get Northern food.

Open: 11 am - 10:30 pm

Address: 34 Race Course Road

KHANSAMA TANDOORI RESTAURANT

This is a really fun place to eat in the evenings. It's very casual, with indoor seating, as well as plastic tables outside, which I prefer. All of the food here is absolutely delicious and there are plenty of vegetarian options available.

Open: 11 am - 2 am

Address: 166 Serangoon Road

MUSTARD

Mustard serves Bengali food, and is known for offering fresh, delicious, and simple food. There's plenty of choice on the menu, but you really can't go wrong. If you're really stuck, I recommend the butter chicken.

Open: 11:30 am - 3 pm, 6-10:45 pm

Address: 32 Race Course Road

OLD CHANG KEE FLAGSHIP

Singapore's iconic curry puffs are the best at their flagship store. Old Chang Kee serves multiple curry puffs, including a vegetarian one, as well as other little snacks. You could come here for a snack or mix and match a few items to make a meal. A curry puff is a Singapore must.

Open: 11 am - 9 pm Mon-Thu, 10 am - 10 pm Fri-Sat, 10 am - 9 pm Sun

Address: 23 Mackenzie Road

♥ MID-RANGE EATS

BRUNCHES CAFE

Brunches Cafe is a cute, vintage-inspired cafe that serves great brunch. It's a great place to go if you feel like sleeping in, grabbing a bite to eat, and having a relaxing day. If you're stopping there in the afternoon, I highly recommend getting truffle fries. Absolutely delicious.

Open: 11 am - 10 pm weekdays, 10 am - 10 pm weekends

Address: 96 Rangoon Road

OLD HEN COFFEE BAR

If you're looking for good coffee, here's a great option! If you're dairy-free, Old Hen offers oat milk, and for those of you who don't drink coffee, they have kombucha (one of the few places in Singapore that does!) and matcha.

Open: 9:30 am - 6:30 pm

Address: 88 Rangoon Road

BANANA LEAF APOLO

Tradition is kept here, with food being served on banana leaves. They're known for their fish head curry, which is a classic Singapore dish. You may or may not have the entire fish head in your bowl, and while that can seem a little bit more out-there, it's perfectly normal - and tasty! They also serve a variety of other Indian food.

Open: 10:30 am - 10:30 pm

Address: 54 Race Course Road

WHAT TO DO IN LITTLE INDIA
BESIDES EAT?

FREE WALKING TOUR

Imma be honest. The only way to absorb the culture, religion and history of Little India is to go on a walking tour with a guide who can explain everything to you! And why wouldn't you? The tour is free and 2.5 hours of fascinating fun.

Contact: There are two companies to check out for free walking tours: Indie Singapore and Monster Day Tours.

Ps. Both of these companies offer free walking tours in other parts of the island that are equally fascinating.

💰 **How Much:** Totally free – but customary to tip whatever you feel ($10-$20 is my suggestion).

Here are some things to expect to see in little India:

📍 SRI VEERAMAKALIAMMAN TEMPLE

One of the most intricate Hindu Temples entrances ever. This temple is dedicated to the Goddess Kali – she is the destroyer of evil. and is a peaceful break from the busy streets of Little India. You can go inside, but make sure you're wearing appropriate clothing!

📍 SRI SRINIVASA PERUMAL TEMPLE

This is one of the oldest temples in Singapore, and it's absolutely beautiful. The incredible entrance piece shows different incarnations of the God Vishnu. This Hindu temple was started in 1855, well before Singapore was its own country!

📍 TAN TENG NIAH

Here is one of the last standing original Chinese homes in this part of Singapore, formerly owned by Tan Teng Niah, a pioneer of the sugarcane and sweets industry in Singapore. The outside of this building is one of the most colorful parts of Little India!

Cost: Free

🕒 **Open:** 24/7

🌐 **Address:** 37 Kerbau Road

📍 TEMPLE OF 1000 LIGHTS

This Buddhist Temple, also called Sakya Muni Buddha Gaya Temple, was set up by the by the renowned Thai monk, Vutthisarain, the 1920s. This 15-metre-high statue of a seated Buddha is one of the most impressive Buddha statues in Singapore.

☞ **FUN FACT**

Northern Indian dishes use more meat and dairy, whereas the Southern Indian dishes have more vegetables and seafood. It's a regional and religious thing. Some regions of India have access to seafood and some don't. Some regions of India don't eat beef (as the cow is sacred) and some love beef!

SHOPPING IN LITTLE INDIA

Shopping in Little India is such an adventure and insanely affordable. My favorite souvenirs to get for my friends back home usually come from Little India, whether its incense, fun snacks, amazing fabrics, or henna! Here's where you go to shop, my love.

TEKKA CENTRE

The Tekka center is a wet market, food hall, and shopping center all in one. I love to eat here when I need something cheap and fast, but I also really like browsing the wet market and picking up some fresh fruit. Their mangos are some of the more affordable, and some of the most delicious, in Singapore. Bring your camera; the colors are amazing!

Cost: Free

Open: 6:30 am - 9 pm

Address: cross streets Bukah Timah & Serangoon Road

MUSTAFA

Leave your boyfriend at the hotel; this place is his worst nightmare. Mustafa is a ginormous complex that sells pretty much everything you could ever want (and many things you never knew you wanted). Their beauty section has it all, from makeup brushes to fake eyelashes…just be weary of the knockoff makeup that is often made with low-quality material. Best of all, Mustafa is open 24/7 (hello, drunk shopping) / 365 days a year.

Open: 24/7

Address: Syed Alwi Road

LITTLE INDIA ARCADE

This is where I like to buy souvenirs to bring home (without spending a fortune). You can buy bangle bracelets, fabrics, henna, and so much more in Little India Arcade. These small shops sell mass homegood but also, intricate hand-crafted treasures.

◎ **Open:** 9 am - 10 pm

⊕ **Address:** 48 Serangoon Road

SERANGOON ROAD

Serangoon Road is a big colorful road full of shophouses that runs through the heart of Little India. I would definitely walk down this road - there are so many shops selling everything you could think of - from fresh fruits to gold jewelry and everything else!

> ☞ **FUN FACT**
>
> Since 1905, Singapore's changed it's time zone 6 times. It's GMT+8 for now.

•••

For more tips, articles, and packing guides—visit my blog at

▶ **TheSoloGirlsTravelGuide.com**

CHAPTER FIVE

Central Business District: ANYTHING BUT STRICTLY BUSINESS

Singapore's Central Business District, also nicknamed the CBD or Financial District by locals, is so much more than the office buildings and skyscrapers within it. The Central Business District goes from near the City Hall MRT down and across the Singapore River, to Raffles Place MRT. This neighborhood borders Chinatown, Bugis, and Marina Bay, so it's super central and a convenient area in which to stay!

WHERE TO STAY IN THE CBD

Because the CBD typically attracts business travelers, most hotels here will be on the mid-range to luxury end. Although the hotels are catered to businessmen and women, you should still consider it because of it's incredibly central location and close proximity to so many other Singapore neighborhoods.

♥ BUDGET

You won't really find budget hotels in the Central Business District, but there are loads on the outskirts of the CBD. I would take a look at some of the hostel recommendations in the Bugis and Chinatown chapters, though here are some nearby that we haven't mentioned yet!

MET A SPACE POD @ BOAT QUAY

This one's for the girls who like to have their own space. The capsule pods give you all the privacy you need while still maintaining that hostel price. The best part about these capsules is that there's a mirror inside each one, so you don't have to trek to the bathroom to do your makeup or brush your hair. This is especially handy because there are loads of bars in Boat Quay – you never know who you'll meet!

♥ **Style:** Dorms

💰 **Starts at:** $52 SGD

⊕ **Where:** Boat Quay

⊕ **Address:** 51 Boat Quay

QUARTERS CAPSULE HOTEL

Located right in the center of Boat Quay, with tons of bars and restaurants in the surrounding area, Quarters Capsule Hotel offers comfortable dorms with retractable blinds for privacy, so you can choose when you want to meet new hostel friends or have a little quiet time. The kitchen and reception area have plenty of bar stools and tables, so it's easy to make new friends to explore with!

- ♥ **Style:** Dorms
- 💰 **Starts at:** $50 SGD
- 🌐 **Where:** Boat Quay
- 🌐 **Address:** 12 Circular Road

RIVER CITY INN

With plenty of bookshelf-lined common areas and travelers passing in and out, this quirky hostel is an incredible place to stay if you're looking to meet others. Stay here if you want to get super social – this hostel is right above all of Boat Quay's bars, and it's just a quick walk to Clarke Quay if you're in the mood to dance until the sun rises.

- ♥ **Style:** Dorms
- 💰 **Starts at:** $27 SGD
- 🌐 **Where:** Boat Quay
- 🌐 **Address:** 33 Hong Kong Street

☞ **FUN FACT**

Singapore is a young country - it only became independent in 1965!

♥ MID-RANGE

Oasia Hotel Downtown

OASIA HOTEL DOWNTOWN

This modern hotel offers plenty of greenery, a beautiful bar, and not one, but TWO rooftop pools. It's a relaxing hotel in the center of Tanjong Pagar and is conveniently located near all the best food spots. Ps. The hotel bar is sexy, inviting and gives you pretty great chances of meeting other travelers once your post up in a bar-side stool.

♥ **Style:** Privates

💰 **Starts at:** $174 SGD / $129 USD

🌐 **Where:** Tanjong Pagar

🌐 **Address:** 100 Peck Seah Street

♥ LUXURY

RAFFLES HOTEL

This is the ultimate luxury hotel in Singapore. This heritage hotel offers beautiful suites that balance the history and classic style of the hotel with modern luxury. The hotel is absolutely stunning, with an outdoor pool and three restaurants. It's also the home of the Long Bar, the bar where the iconic Singapore Sling cocktail was created!

♥ **Style:** Private suites

💰 **Starts at:** $1620 SGD

🌐 **Where:** near Esplanade MRT

🌐 **Address:** 1 Beach Road

CARLTON HOTEL

Come for the upscale rooms, stay for the pool, gym, and breakfast buffet! At this hotel, it's all about the little things- the amazing rain showers, the spot-on recommendations from staff, and the plethora of restaurants just a few minutes away. Too tired from exploring to go out for dinner? Their in-house restaurants are excellent.

♥ **Style:** Privates

💰 **Starts at:** $207 SGD / $153 USD

🌐 **Where:** in between Bugis and the CBD

🌐 **Address:** 76 Bras Basah Road

SWISSOTEL THE STAMFORD

The best part about this hotel is the size of the rooms. Singapore's small, and a lot of the hotel rooms are too! Not here! There's plenty of room to stretch out and to have some space to call your own, but you're still in the center of the Central Business District. Connected to the Raffles Place Mall, you're just a stone throw away from Singaporean food, loads of shopping, and the MRT.

♥ **Style:** Privates

💰 **Starts at:** $255 SGD

🌐 **Where:** Heart of the CBD

🌐 **Address:** 2 Stamford Road

THE CAPITOL KEMPINSKI

This 5-star hotel is located in an old heritage building but is surprisingly modern. With nods to the building's history, this modern hotel is the ultimate place to stay if you want to balance old and new. The pool, spa, and bars are incredible, and because the hotel is so close to City Hall MRT, you can come back to rest in the middle of the day and then hit the town again for some nightlife.

♥ **Style:** Privates

💰 **Starts at:** $289 SGD

🌐 **Where:** Heart of the CBD, next to City Hall MRT

🌐 **Address:** 15 Stamford Road

WHERE TO EAT IN THE CBD

Restaurants in the Central Business District is usually catered towards professionals who either need a quick but delicious lunch, or a nicer place to bring colleagues for dinner. There are plenty of places to eat no matter what your budget.

♥ BUDGET

LAU PA SAT FOOD COMPLEX

Even if you aren't on a budget, this is a must-eat place. Also known as Telok Ayer Market, Lau Pa Sat brings plenty of different cuisines and tons of local Singaporean dishes to a beautiful hawker center. It's a beautiful complex, with an open Victorian-style architecture, and all of the food here is absolutely delicious.

Open: 24/7, though it's best to go during meal hours for most options!

Address: 18 Raffles Quay

BOON TAT STREET

Mondays-Fridays at 7pm, Boon Tat Street (literally behind Lau Pa Sat) closes down to cars and in an instant, turns into a food street! Plastic tables are set out and fill up instantly with locals and tourists who have come to eat meat and shrimp on a stick! There are dozens of satay BBQ spots grilling over an open flame. Order a set, take a ticket, have a seat, order some beers and your food will be bright to you. Ask for the chili sauce!

> **PRO TIP**
> Bring wet tissues in your purse.

Open: Monday-Friday at 7pm

IRVIN'S SALTED EGG

This isn't technically a restaurant, but it sells Singapore's favorite snack! Salted egg chips and fish skin became SUPER popular a few years ago. I know, I know. Salted egg fish skin doesn't sound super appetizing. But don't knock it until you try it!

⊙ **Open:** 10 am - 7:30 pm weekdays, 10 am - 2:30 pm on Saturday. Closed Sunday.

⊕ **Address:** Raffles Xchange, Basement 1

FOOD JUNCTION @ ONE RAFFLES PLACE

Food Junction is a food court designed for the working man (and woman) which offers fast and yummy food. Just like a food court back home but with an Asian twist (duh). My favorite here is the chicken rice.

⊙ **Open:** 8 am - 9 pm, closed weekends

⊕ **Address:** 1 Raffles Place

FOOD JUNCTION @ RAFFLES CITY

Again, Food Junction does not disappoint. At Raffles City, my go-to is the da xiao mian – which is thick knife-cut noodles in an amazingly flavorful beef broth. This location is open on Saturdays!

⊙ **Open:** 8 am - 9 pm weekdays, 8 am - 6 pm Saturdays. Closed Sundays.

⊕ **Address:** 252 North Bridge Rd, #03-15/16/17

♥ MID-RANGE

MELLOWER COFFEE

This spot has become Instagram famous for their drink, Sweet Little Rain. You're served an americano with a puff of cotton candy hanging above it. The steam melts the cotton candy, and sugar water drops into your Americano.

◉ **Open:** 8 am - 10 pm

⊕ **Address:** 108 Middle Road

CHIJMES

This beautiful historic building used to be an old Christian convent, but today, this beautiful white complex stands out in Singapore as a great place to eat. The complex is home to a collection of gourmet restaurants and bars. Ones to try: Carnivore, Indochine, and Ashino.

◉ **Open:** 24/7 but restaurants have their own hours

⊕ **Address:** 30 Victoria Street

FLOCK CAFE SG

Flock Cafe has all-day breakfast, pastas, and burgers. What else could you want? I love their waffles and their pancakes, but if you who don't have such a big sweet tooth, their chicken katsu burger is heavenly.

◉ **Open:** 8 am - 9:30 pm

⊕ **Address:** 1-25 Tiong Bahru Estate

THE PROVIDORE

The Providore has floor to ceiling windows that overlook Raffles Place. Grab a coffee and admire the view or stuff your face with a hearty breakfasts or lunch. Their lobster mac & cheese and crab linguine are favorites, although they also have healthier options available like the organic quinoa salad!

◉ **Open:** 8 am - 10:30 pm weekdays, 8 am - 10 pm on Saturdays, 9 am - 6 pm on Sundays

⊕ **Address:** 7 Raffles Place

CHICKEN UP KOREAN RESTAURANT

Fried chicken and soju, anyone? While this place specializes in Korean fried chicken (which is all the rage in Singapore) they also have rice and noodle dishes that hit the spot.

Open: 5:30 pm - 2 am Sun-Thu, 5:30 pm - 3 am Fri, 5:30 pm - 12 am Sat

Address: 48 Tanjong Pagar Road

♥ LUXURY

ONE ALTITUDE

To access One Altitude, you'll need to take an elevator 282 meters up into the sky! Inside, there's an incredible dining room that serves great steak meals, and on the rooftop, there's a fun bar and club...with one of the best views in town.

Open: 6 pm - 2 am Sun-Tues, Thurs, 6 pm - 4 pm Wed, Fri, & Sat

Address: One Raffles Place

THE BLACK SWAN

The Black Swan is located inside a stunning 1930s landmark building and is a popular place to come for a set lunch menu. In the evening, come for oysters and wine. They've got large plates with seafood, red meat, and all the fancy fixin's for a special night out on the town.

Open: 11:30 am - 11 pm Mon & Tues, 11:30 am - 11:30 pm Wed-Fri, 5:30-11 pm Sat, closed Sundays

Address: 19 Cecil Street

FLUTES

Flutes is located in the National Gallery of Singapore and is inspired by its location. It's held in the part of the museum that opened to commemorate Queen Victoria, so it's menu is European-inspired. They also offer an afternoon tea, which is a wonderful way to finish up a trip to the museum.

Open: 11:30 am - 2 pm & 6:30-10 pm weekdays, 10:30 am - 2:30 pm & 6:30-10:30 pm Saturdays, 10:30 am - 5 pm Sundays.

Address: 93 Stamford Road

WHAT TO DO IN THE CBD

Most of Singapore's best museums are located within or right next to the CBD!

NATIONAL GALLERY

The National Gallery is a museum full of Southeast Asian art. While you can explore freely on your own, I highly recommend taking advantage of the museum's free tours! There's so much more to the art than meets the eye! An English-speaking guide will give you a deep dive into these masterpieces, plus the history of Singapore as it related to each work of art.

Cost: $20 SGD

Open: 10 am - 7 pm daily, with extended hours until 9 pm on Fridays.

Address: 1 St Andrews Road

Tour Information: You'll have to book these ahead of time – at least 20 minutes ahead of the tour time.

Tour Options

- **Building Highlights Tour:** 11 am daily with an extra 3 pm tour on weekends
- **DBS Singapore Gallery Highlights Tour:** 1 pm daily with an extra 2:30 pm tour on weekends
- **UOB Southeast Asia Gallery Highlights Tour:** 3:30 pm daily
- **Highlights of Lim Cheng Hoe, Painting Singapore Tour:** 11:30 am Fri-Sun (I recommend this one!)
- **Highlights of the Gallery Tour:** Weekends at 4 pm

NATIONAL GALLERY BACK OF HOUSE TOUR

This is a tour I recommend if you're interested in Singapore's legal system and secrets (which is quite fascinating no matter who you are)! Located in the National Gallery, this tour takes you into the restricted areas, leading you through hidden passages and trapdoors to the former courthouse. You even get to hear about some of the cases tried in the courtroom, too!

Ticket Cost: $15 SGD on top of the $20 SGD National Gallery Ticket

Tour Information: Friday at 5:30 pm, Saturday at 3:30 pm.

⊕ **Address:** 1 St Andrews Road

PERANAKAN MUSEUM

Peranakan culture is an important part of Singapore. Peranakan refers to an ethnic group of Chinese that settled in the Malaysian archipelago. Here, there are touches of Dutch, Portuguese, and British cultures, as well, because #colonization. This museum highlights the tangled culture and turbulent history of this group.

Ticket Cost: $10 SGD

⊙ **Hours:** Currently under renovation

⊕ **Address:** 39 Armenian Street

SINGAPORE ART MUSEUM

This museum houses amazing contemporary art. The museum is beautiful, so even if you aren't planning on entering the museum, check out the grounds surrounding the building itself (with a bubble tea in hand). Inside the museum, you'll find works of art from Asian (specifically Southeast Asian), artists.

⊙ **Hours:** Currently under renovation, but there are SAM exhibits around Singapore.

⊕ **Address:** 8 Queen Street

FORT CANNING PARK

Fort Canning Park is a beautiful place to walk through. It's located on a hill and there's so much greenery. It's a great place to escape the feeling of being right in the middle of a city. I recommend grabbing some food and having a picnic in the park!

Cost: Free!

⊙ **Hours:** 24/7

⊕ **Address:** River Valley Road

SHOPPING IN THE CBD

Bougie shopping at its best. The CBD is all about those malls, baby.

RAFFLES CITY SHOPPING CENTER

Birkenstock. Calvin Cline. Chanel. Coach. Gucci. You get the pictures. Raffles City is one of the more upscale malls, with high street stores for you fancy people and a basement food court for you hungry people. And there's a McDonalds. Halleluiah.

◔ **Open:** 10 am - 10 pm

⊕ **Address:** 252 North Bridge Road

CAPITOL PIAZZA

Modern and airy with a glass ceiling and plenty of places to eat. Capitol Piazza is a place to stroll, window shop and stop by the iconic Parisian chain, Angelina, for some of the best hot chocolate ever. And don't worry, it's air-conditioned, so ordering hot chocolate in Singapore isn't as crazy as it sounds.

◔ **Open:** 10:30 am – 10:30 pm

⊕ **Address:** 13 Stamford Road

FUNAN MALL + MOVIE THEATER

All the techy and digital goods can be found here in Funan mall. Buy a new phone, get a new charger, invest in a selfie stick. There's also a movie theater here!

Movie times: Capitaland.com/sg/malls/funan/en

◔ **Open:** 10 am - 10 pm daily, closing at 10:45 on Saturdays

⊕ **Address:** 107 North Bridge Road

CHAPTER SIX

Other Places in Singapore

This wouldn't be a Singapore guide if I didn't mention some of these neighborhoods less traveled, too! From adventurous Sentosa to luxurious Orchard to the hidden gem of Tiong Bahru – here is your "off the beaten path" neighborhoods that tourists usually don't make it to...but are certainly worth a visit if you have time!

CLARKE QUAY

Clarke Quay is where I'd point anyone looking for a good time. Clarke Quay is situated right on the Singapore River. Whilst super sleepy during the day, it truly comes alive at night. Restaurants get full, clubs and bars start to open, and people come out to play. It's popular with both expats and locals, and you're bound to have a good time here. It's also covered, so if it's raining, don't worry! You can still come here, and you won't have to worry about getting wet. Here are some of the best evening activities in Clarke Quay.

SINGAPORE RIVER CRUISE

This is a must in Singapore! The Singapore River Cruise starts in Clarke Quay and takes you on the river, into Marina Bay. The boat itself is super cute, and the views from the boat ride are fantastic. It takes around 40 minutes.

Cost: $25

G-MAX REVERSE BUNGY & GIANT SWING

This, to be blunt, is fucking scary. Unless you're a thrill seeker, that is. The reverse bungy is essentially a ride that catapults you into the air. Pro: You get a view of the Singapore River from high up. Con: You probably won't see much because you'll be bouncing around in the air. The giant swing is less scary, but you're still really high and swooping through the air at a high speed.

Cost: $45 for one, $65 for both.

NIGHT ON THE TOWN

As you'll see in the next chapter, "Nightlife in Singapore", Clarke Quay is the hotspot for getting a little tipsy. Happy hours, live music, clubs, and more. Here is where the international crowd of expats, bougie travelers, and locals who like to party come in mix and mingle til mid-morning hours.

SENTOSA

Where adventure and relaxation meet! Sentosa is an tropical little island right off the coast of Singapore. On Sentosa, you can be super adventurous with go ziplining or indoor skydiving; or you can go to a beach club and sip cocktails under the sun.

You can get there by a tram from Vivo City (Harbor-front MRT), or you can walk along the promenade over to Sentosa. I prefer walking, as you get a beautiful view of the water.

THINGS TO DO ON SENTOSA

IFLY

Ever want to go skydiving, without the whole jumping-out-of-a-plane part? iFly is a good compromise. There's a giant air tube and you suit up and jump in to experience what skydiving feels like. It's super fun and surprisingly active.

How Much: $89 SGD for one skydive, $119 for 2

UNIVERSAL STUDIOS

Universal Studios in Singapore is a great way to get out of the city and have some fun. It's great year-round, but during Halloween, they have an incredibly scary Asian-horror inspired Halloween Horror Nights, which is absolutely terrifying.

How Much: $79 SGD

VISIT A SPA

While on one side of Sentosa has all of the beach clubs and amusement parks, there's another, more hidden side of Sentosa, where people live, and luxury hotels are. These luxury hotels often have spa treatments you can book without being a guest and being able to go into a more exclusive part of Singapore and getting pampered is a fantastic way to really feel like you're on an exotic holiday.

TANJONG BEACH CLUB

Tanjong Beach Club is where you should definitely go if you want a beach day. Singapore's beaches are man-made, so they don't exactly have that amazing tropical island beauty. Tanjong Beach Club is a spot where you can rent a day bed on the beach and also use their pool. Food and drinks can be pricey, but the experience is great. It can be a really lively, cocktail-fueled day, or a relaxing lounging day.

CONTINENTAL ASIA'S MOST SOUTHERN POINT

Along the beach, you'll find a small bridge that takes you to Continental Asia's Most Southern Point. There's a sign where you can take a picture, and definitely go if you're near, but don't go out of your way to see this.

S.E.A AQUARIUM

This is a huge aquarium. It has over 1,000 species of marine life and is totally worth a visit if you love sea life. The tanks are giant, and you really get to see so much more than you'd expect. There are also extra activities you can pay for, like swimming with sharks and getting your SCUBA license.

How Much: $40 SGD

TRICK EYE MUSEUM

The trick eye museum is super fun if you like 3D art. It's really interactive, so bring a tripod or be ready to ask someone to take photos of you!

MEGA ADVENTURE SINGAPORE

There are plenty of fun activities here. You can go on a bungee trampoline, do a treetop obstacle course, zipline, or bungee jump! You can do one of the activities or choose a package of multiple.

How Much: $15 for the bungee trampoline, $18 for the bungee jump, $$37 for the treetop obstacle course, and $55 for the zipline.

> **FUN FACT**
> Bordering Singapore's mainland, there are 63 other islands that make up the country of Singapore.

For more tips, articles, and packing guides—visit my blog at
▶ TheSoloGirlsTravelGuide.com

TIONG BAHRU

Tiong Bahru is the beautiful Singapore neighborhood established in the 1920s, making it one of Singapore's oldest housing estates. While some may still think of it as a sleepy part of Singapore, it's become a really trendy, hipster, kind of neighborhood that is full of some of Singapore's best-kept hidden gems.

THINGS TO DO IN TIONG BAHRU

TIONG BAHRU BAKERY

This bakery is incredibly well known across Singapore. Their French pastries are incredibly flaky and buttery. I love the lemon tart, where you can choose your level of tartness, but I also love coming here for a pastry and coffee to start my day.

⊙ **Open:** 8 am - 8 pm

⊕ **Address:** 56 Eng Hoon Street

BOOKS ACTUALLY

Books Actually is such a sweet little shop. It's focused on Singaporean literature and has the best selection of books, stationery, and other little knick-knacks. This is where I'd go if I needed a nice souvenir for someone special, or for the bookworm in your life.

CURATED RECORDS

Curated Records is definitely a place to go if you love hunting for amazing treasures. Vinyl records are hard to find in Singapore, but Curated Records has over 2000 of them. It's an extensive collection of amazing bands and artists that you might not otherwise discover.

STREET ART

Tiong Bahru is filled with some beautiful murals. They appear in places you wouldn't expect - next to windows in residential areas, on the sides of homes, and in little corners. Get lost in Tiong Bahru and keep your eyes open for some of these amazing murals.

FORTY HANDS

Forty Hands is what started the artisan coffee movement in Singapore. This is an incredible place for brunch or lunch, with so many different options to choose from. Their eggs benedict is my go-to. Definitely get a coffee with your food!

⊙ **Hours:** 7 am - 6 pm weekdays, 7:30 pm - 7 pm weekends

⊕ **Address:** 78 Yong Siak St

ORCHARD

Orchard is one of the craziest shopping streets you'll see in Singapore, but it is an amazing place to go on a rainy day or if you want to shop! The area is made up of over 20 different shopping malls and there are soooo many luxury stores within them. You can also find high-street shops and more affordable, local trendy clothes, along with plenty of food options and anything else you could imagine! Some of the malls are connected by underground passages and it's quite easy to get lost within the shops.

THINGS TO DO IN ORCHARD

ION ORCHARD

ION Orchard is a super modern mall that has eight floors of shopping. The more affordable food is in the basement level, and the higher-end places to eat are on levels 2 and 3. I recommend going up to ION Sky - it's on level 56 of the building and there are sweeping views of Singapore from the observation deck. To get to ION Sky, go to the concierge on Level 4. Orchard MRT is on the bottom floor with the food.

> ☞ **FUN FACT**
>
> Singapore's Istana (near Orchard), where the president lives, is open to the public 5 days a year! The second day of Chinese New Year, Labor Day, Hari Raya Puasa, National Day, and Deepavali.

313 SOMERSET

313 Somerset has plenty of shopping and places to eat (including a Cold Stone Creamery!). It's really easy to access this mall because the Somserset MRT is located in the basement. I really like coming to the Library@Orchard, a really modern library with an absurd amount of books. The travel section has so many guidebooks, which are great to look at if you're planning your adventures after Singapore.

PARAGON SHOPPING CENTER

Paragon is a little bit more of an upscale mall. If you're looking for nicer, higher-end clothing, this is a good place to look! The reason I go to Paragon most often is that their Din Tai Fung location is one of the less-busy locations! Din Tai Fung has the best soup dumplings and I highly recommend it!

LUCKY PLAZA

Lucky Plaza is where international workers go to send money back to their home countries and where you can find cheap goods. Not too many people come here to shop, but Lucky Plaza is a bit of a hidden gem. There are plenty of tour operators in Lucky Plaza and they offer bundled attraction tickets that will end up being cheaper than paying for each attraction individually. Definitely worth a visit if you're planning on going to Singapore's top sights, but skip it on a Sunday, when it's the most crowded.

FAR EAST PLAZA

Far East Plaza is a fabulous mall if you're trying to find cheap and trendy fashion items. It's also where a lot of people go to get piercings and tattoos. The basement is where you'll find all of the trendy shops - you can find clothing and shoes here, though they do run a little small because it's Asian sizing!

GET AN ICE CREAM SANDWICH!

On Orchard road, in between ION Orchard and 313 Somerset, there will be people selling ice cream sandwiches. They are literally sandwiches. Ice cream sandwiched between a large piece of white bread. The bread is usually colored pink and green, and it tastes like normal bread. It's definitely not for everyone, but it's less than $2 SGD and it's a novelty Singapore snack!

CHAPTER SEVEN

Nightlife in Singapore

While you can find bars and happy hours all over Singapore, here is where to look when you wanna let your hair down and get a little wild...cause you're on vacation.

CAFE IGUANA (CLARKE QUAY)

This is my pick for Mexican food & tequila shots in Singapore. The margaritas are great - mango is my favorite! It has a really fun and lively atmosphere.

CHUPITOS (CLARKE QUAY)

This is my absolute favorite place to head to before the clubs. Chupitos is a shots bar and the shots are super fun, tasty, and some of them are quite... mischievous. The shooters are really fun - Paddle Pop is my favorite and truly tastes like a Paddle Pop! Appletini and Pandan cake are close seconds. Go during ladies night (Wednesday) for a free third shot with the shooters.

F.CLUB X ATTICA (CLARKE QUAY)

F.Club x Attica is a club complex made up of two rooms - the Ruby Club, which plays hip-hop, R&B, and chart remixes, and the White

Lounge, which plays tech and house. In between them, there's an outdoor courtyard where you can get some fresh air or have a smoke.

$20 SGD before midnight (go before, get your re-entry stamp, and come back when it's lively!). I recommend going on Wednesdays, ladies' night, so you get free entry and 5 free drinks! Alcohol is expensive in Singapore, so definitely take advantage of ladies' night!

ZOUK SINGAPORE (CLARKE QUAY)

Zouk is an iconic club. Plenty of locals and travelers flock here on the weekends looking to drink and dance. If a big international DJ is making an appearance in Singapore, I'll bet you they'll be playing a set at Zouk. Zouk itself is made up of four clubs - Zouk, Phuture, Velvet Underground Lounge, and Velvet Underground Dance - as well as a wine bar.

Music: Zouk - techno, house, trance; Phuture: hip hop/R&B

Cost: $25 for ladies, including 2 drinks

Minimum Age: 18, but for Velvet Underground, 21.

⊙ **Hours:** vary, but I wouldn't show up until 11 pm or midnight!

1 ALTITUDE (MARINA BAY)

1 Altitude stays open until the early hours of the morning, with amazing views of the most iconic skyline in Singapore. Bring your dancing shoes!

Cost: $25

⊕ **Address:** 1 Raffles Place

CE LA VIE (MARINA BAY)

While most people know Ce La Vie as the luxurious dining experience at the top of Marina Bay, it doubles as a club! Come here to meet other tourists and expats – this is a social place to be! And pro tip: come after 10pm on Wednesdays for free entry on ladies night! It's also free on Sunday-Tuesday and Thursday, but don't expect to see a ton of people around. The party really starts on Wednesday, Fridays, and Saturdays. You'll have to pay a cover charge on Fridays and Saturdays, which varies depending on the event and DJ. Expect to pay around $30.

⊕ **Address:** 1 Bayfront Avenue, Tower 3

BANG BANG NIGHTCLUB (MARINA BAY)

Located at the base of the Pan-Pacific hotel, this club is popular with business travelers and people in their 30s. This is a great place to go for lots of dancing and fun – there's a platform above the main floor where you can dance, and for the bold gals, there's a cage with a pole to dance in. RSVP ahead of time for free ladies night entry!

⊕ **Address:** 7 Raffles Boulevard

28 HONG KONG STREET (CBD)

This bar's made the World's Top 50 bar list! The bar is home to an incredible juxtaposition between the old shophouse exterior, and swanky, modern, and luxurious interior. The drinks are all creative and one of a kind, inspired by different cities.

⊕ **Address:** 28 Hong Kong Street

⊙ **Hours:** 6 pm – 2 am Monday-Thursday, 6 pm – 3 am Fridays & Saturdays, closed Sundays.

ATLAS SINGAPORE (BUGIS)

This is one of the most stunning bars I've ever seen. A floor to ceiling shelf of gin and champagne are the main attraction here, though you can definitely drink more than gin and champagne here! The cocktails are all delightful and so carefully thought out and paired. Sitting in the velvet chairs, sipping a cocktail truly feels like you've entered a Gatsby party.

OPERATION DAGGER (CHINATOWN)

This speakeasy is little difficult to find – the entrance is a plain glass door and there's a little staircase leading you downstairs inside. The outside may not look like anything special, but the bar is sleek and modern. The cocktails are the best part of this speakeasy – you order according to flavors instead of ingredients. This results in an amazing sensory experience and you get to really focus on the taste of the drink.

⊙ **Hours:** 6 pm – 12 am, closed Sundays

⊕ **Address:** 7 Ann Siang Hill

CHAPTER EIGHT
Changi Airport

The world's best airport; officially. Changi Airport consistently wins award after award for being one of the best airports in the world due to its design, amenities, shopping, eating...all of it. Changi Airport is so advanced and entertaining, that locals will come and spend the day at the airport as if it were Universal Studios or somethin'. With a butterfly garden, swimming pool, movie theatre and more...it makes sense.

That being said, Changi Airport is an adventure in itself; one that you can explore on a long layover or do what I recommend which is this: come to the airport 5 hours before your flight and take full advantage this one-of-a-kind airport adventure.

HOW TO GET TO THE AIRPORT

BY MRT

To get to Changi, hop on the East-West MRT line. It's the green line when you're looking at the MRT map. From City Hall/Raffles Place, it takes about 45 minutes to get to the airport. Though it's rare to have to wait more than 5 minutes for the MRT, I'd leave an hour before you want to arrive at the airport just in case. And hey, more time at Changi Airport certainly isn't a bad thing!

You'll arrive in Terminal 2 and tickets cost around $2 SGD.

BY TAXI

Taxis are the fastest way to get to the airport. It only takes around 20-30 minutes from the central part of Singapore, and they drop you off right at the terminal you're flying from. If you have loads of luggage, I recommend taking a taxi so you don't have to walk to the MRT. It's super easy, but they cost around $30, and more if you're going during a peak time. If you're going during peak time, check out Grab taxis, as they can sometimes be cheaper!

BY GRAB

Grab taxis are easy to get anywhere in Singapore. Just download the app, enter the airport as your destination, and wait to be picked up! These are roughly $30 SGD and they can take you directly to the terminal you need to get to.

WHERE TO EAT IN THE AIRPORT

STRAIT'S FOOD VILLAGE

This is the best place to eat before a flight or if you're landing late. It's just like any other mall food court in Singapore, with affordable prices and plenty of options. I love the duck rice here but there are plenty of stalls, so pick and choose a few things to eat!

🌐 **Located in** Terminal 3

DIN TAI FUNG

Din Tai Fung is one of the most famous restaurants in Asia and is a Singapore staple. The food is traditional Taiwanese cuisine, known best for their xiao long bao and the spicy noodles. Xiao long bao are soup dumplings – they're light dumplings filled with perfectly seasoned meat and broth. They melt in your mouth and are a serious must-eat. But watch out! The soup can be super hot! The spicy noodles are fresh the death as everything here is made from scratch! Located in JEWEL

CRAVE - THE ORIGINAL ADAM ROAD NASI LEMAK BY SELERA RASA

You CAN'T leave Singapore without trying Nasi Lemak!!! This coconut rice-based dish is to die for. It's fragrant, sweet and salty, and so rich, yet also light. It's indescribable. This location is made with the same recipe as the Adam Road nasi lemak stall, arguably the best place to get nasi lemak.

🌐 **Located in** terminals 2 & 3 to the public, and in transit terminal 2

ALOHA POKE

Want to eat something healthy before a long flight? Come to Aloha Poke. These poke bowls are fresh and flavorful. The spicy tuna has just the right amount of spice and you can choose so many good veggies and toppings to put in your bowl.

🌐 **Located in** JEWEL Level 5

4 FINGERS CRISPY CHICKEN

Korean fried chicken is incredibly trendy in Singapore. Try this, and you'll understand why. As the name suggests, the fried chicken is super crispy, never soggy (ew), perfectly salted, and of course, best eaten with a side of fries.

🌐 **Located in** Terminal 3 and in terminal 1 transit.

AN ACAI AFFAIR

With all of Singapore's sweet tropical fruit, it would be a shame NOT to get an acai bowl! Sweetened just with fresh fruit, acai bowls are healthy pre-flight snacks or light meal before your long-haul.

🌐 **Located in** JEWEL B2

JUMBO SEAFOOD

Here's your last chance to try chili crab and black pepper crab before leaving Singapore. These are some of Singapore's most well-known dishes, and they're absolutely delicious. The chili crab is salty, not too spicy, and decadent to eat. The black pepper crab is an explosion of black pepper, but in the best way – it even gets a little spicy!

🌐 **Located in** JEWEL Level 3

• •

For more tips, articles, and packing guides—visit my blog at

▶ **TheSoloGirlsTravelGuide.com**

THINGS TO DO IN CHANGI AIRPORT

These are just "things to keep you un-bored". The adventures in Changi Airport are out of this world. This is why millions of people every year intentionally book a layover in Changi Airport. Let me just scratch the surface...

INSIDE THE TERMINAL

BUTTERFLY GARDEN

The Butterfly Garden is an area where you can walk around, and butterflies fly all around you. It's a great way to stretch your legs before or after a long flight.

🌐 **Located in** Terminal 3

SUNFLOWER GARDEN

The Sunflower Garden is a wonderful way to feel like you're getting out of the airport. It's a wonderful little walk and it's beautiful!

🌐 **Located in** Terminal 2

CACTUS GARDEN

The Cactus Garden makes you feel like you're out of Singapore! Wander around and enjoy being in nature and out of your airplane seat.

🌐 **Located in** Terminal 1

ORCHID GARDEN

Orchids are Singapore's national flower, so naturally, Changi Airport would have an Orchid garden! These flowers are super beautiful and delicate, and it's amazing to be surrounded by them in an airport!

🌐 **Located in** Terminal 2

ROOFTOP SWIMMING POOL

If you have a long layover, this is the place to go. Inside the airport hotel, there's a rooftop swimming pool. It costs $17 to go into for the day but is well worth it if you need to relax between flights.

Hours; 6 am - 12 am

⊕ **Located in** Terminal 1

MOVIE THEATRES

There are free movie theatres playing newly released blockbusters in Changi. This is a great place to go if you need to take a quick nap, but it's also great if you've wanted to see a new movie!

⊕ **Two locations** in Terminal 2 and 3

RELAX WITH A MASSAGE

Free massage? Yes please! These foot massage chairs are sprinkled all throughout the terminals. Need something a little more intense?

⊕ There's a spa in Terminal 1

OUTSIDE THE TERMINAL

JEWEL

Singapore's latest addition to Changi Airport is INSANE. JEWEL is considered as its own wing of the airport – but is most famous for the Instagram-famous waterfall located in the Forest Valley. But the adventure doesn't stop at the waterfall. Inside JEWEL, there's a hedge maze, a bouncing net, a big trampoline-esque walkway, and the canopy bridge; a bridge that gives you an aerial view of Jewel. There's also. Come hungry - some of Changi's best restaurants are located here.

KINETIC RAIN

Kinetic Rain is an art installation made up of hundreds of metal raindrops. They move slowly to create different pictures and shapes, at one point, arranging themselves into an airplane.

⊕ **Located in** Terminal 1

THE SLIDE

The Slide is the largest slide in Singapore. It loops from Level 1 down to Basement 3. If you spend $10 in one receipt, you can exchange the receipt for a free slide down. Show them your receipt at the Level 1 Information desk in terminal 3.

⊕ **Located in** Terminal 3

☞ **FUN FACT**

The Rain Vortex in Jewel at Changi Airport is the world's largest indoor waterfall.

For more tips, articles, and packing guides—visit my blog at

▶ **TheSoloGirlsTravelGuide.com**

WHERE TO SLEEP IN CHANGI AIRPORT

It's pretty common to find travelers sleeping on the floor or cramped in between gate seats at most airports, but that's not how it rolls at Changi. In Singapore's airport, there are a few different options for getting some shut-eye. Hell, you might even wake up refreshed!

SNOOZE LOUNGES — TERMINALS 1, 3 & 4

These lounges are a great place to rest and sleep if you don't want to pay for a hotel room. They have plenty of chairs to sleep in – while they don't lie flat, they're super comfortable and they're reclined enough that you can doze off during your layover. There are outlets located at each lounge chair, too, so you don't have to worry about running out of battery.

> **PRO TIP**
>
> Keep your passports and boarding passes ready! If you're staying overnight at the airport, security guards will wake you up to make sure you have onward travel arrangements and aren't just bummin' it in the airport.

AEROTEL AIRPORT TRANSIT HOTEL — TERMINAL 1

A hotel inside the airport – best for those super long layovers. Each room has a full bathroom with showers, and you have access to a pool and jacuzzi with poolside bar. Where else can you spend a layover in a jacuzzi?! These are comfortable rooms perfect for relaxing in between exploring Changi's attractions. Best part? They are pretty affordable! Standard rooms start at $100 SGD, and budget rooms start at $60.

⊕ **Located** above gate D41

AMBASSADOR TRANSIT HOTEL — TERMINALS 2 & 3

Hotel room and a shower; what more do you need! They also provide wake-up call services, which is especially handy if you have an early flight. There are two hotels for terminal 2 and 3. Terminal 2 has budget rooms and standard rooms, whereas terminal 3 only has standard rooms.

Standard rooms start at $100 SGD and budget rooms start at $60 SGD.

⊕ Terminal 2 hotel located above the Orchard Garden, and the Terminal 3 hotel is located next to the movie theatre.

JETQUAY SUITES — JETQUAY CIP TERMINAL

These are pay by the hour hotel suites and they all have a garden view! There are only four of these suites, so if you want to stay in one, book early! When you book the suite, you also gain access to the lounge, a shower, and a free meal. You have to stay for a minimum of 6 hours and there's only 1 person allowed per room – perfect for the solo traveler!

Check in between 10 am and 10 pm - $80
Check in between 10 pm and 10 am - $100

Extension per hour: $15

⊕ **Located in** the JetQuay CIT Terminal

☞ **FUN FACT**

Orchids are the national flower of Singapore - you can find them at Changi airport!

PAY PER USE LOUNGES

PLAZA PREMIUM LOUNGE — TERMINAL 1

This lounge has a place to shower and free Singaporean food. If you just need to freshen up, you can pay for just a shower and a welcome drink. And if you just need a place to sleep, you can rent a private resting suite and get 3 hours of lounge access.

⊕ **Located in** terminal 1, level 3 above gate C1

Cost: 5 Hours: $58, 10 Hours: $105. Shower & welcome drink: $16. Private resting suite: $75

AMBASSADOR TRANSIT LOUNGE — TERMINAL 2 & 3

Come to this lounge for a gym to stretch your legs, showers, printers, and workstations, as well as the usual food and drink access. There are also beauty and massage services, as well as private napping suites.

⊕ **Located in** terminal 2, level 3, above the Orchid garden, and in Terminal 3, level 3, near the movie theater.

Cost: $58.85 per 5 hours

THE HAVEN BY JETQUAY (PUBLIC AREA — BEFORE YOU CHECK IN!)

This is the only lounge open to the public – perfect if you have a super early flight but want to take public transport to the airport. There are 18 nap rooms and 13 shower rooms here, and then, of course, the lounge. The lounge has complimentary snacks and beverages, meeting rooms, and a business area.

⊕ **Located in** Terminal 3, Level 1, near DFS Wine & Spirits

Cost:
- Showers from 10 am – 10 pm: $18.83, Showers from 10 pm – 10 am: $23.54,
- Lounge Use 10 am – 10 pm: $37.66 (2 hours), $55.32 (5 hours), $72.97 (8 hours),
- Lounge Use 10 pm – 10 am: $44.73 (2 hours), $62.38 (5 hours), $80.04 (8 hours)
- Nap Rooms 10 am – 10 pm: $88.28 for 3 hours, with a surcharge of $17.66 per hour after
- Nap Rooms 10 pm – 10 am: $100.05 for 3 hours, with a surcharge of $17.66 per hour after

BLOSSOM PREMIUM LOUNGE — TERMINAL 4

This lounge has light food and beverages, as well as showers and an area to have massages, manicures, and pedicures! I can't think of a better way to start a day travelling than with a massage and mani-pedi.

Located in terminal 4, level 2M, near Cheers

Cost: $58

CHANGI LOUNGE — JEWEL

This is the spot for business travelers. There's super fast wifi, a business area, and you can rent a meeting room. There are also showers and napping spaces to freshen up before or after your flight.

Located in Changi JEWEL, Level 1

Cost: $38 (3 hours, lounge only), $50 (3 hours, lounge with shower)

☞ PRO TIP FOR FREQUENT TRAVELERS

Travel with a Priority Pass Card which gives you access to lounges all over the world. I get my Priority Pass Card via my American Express Platinum Card. Visit my blog and search "Credit Card" to learn how that all works!

For more tips, articles, and packing guides—visit my blog at

▶ **TheSoloGirlsTravelGuide.com**

Itineraries for SINGAPORE

Most travelers come to Singapore for a weekend layover and want to make the most of it. I've got an itinerary for that.

Most people will tell actually you that Singapore's only good for two or three days...and even though I disagree and would say that there's actually enough to keep you busy (and happy) for at least a week... I've got an itinerary for it all.

Here are a few realistic itineraries that will leave you feeling inspired, not exhausted!

☞ **WANT ME TO PLAN YOUR TRIP FOR YOU?**
TheSoloGirlsTravelGuide.com

WEEKEND ITINERARY — BACKPACKER EXPERIENCE

♥ **DAY 1: CHINATOWN & MARINA BAY**

- Fly into Changi Airport
- Drop your stuff off at Beary Best Hostel in Chinatown
- Walk to Marina Bay.
- Explore Marina Bay! Head towards the Helix Bridge and into The Shoppes @ Marina Bay for some air conditioning.
- Continue onto Gardens by the Bay - don't miss the supertrees (especially cool at night!).

♥ **DAY 2: SINGAPORE'S NEIGHBORHOODS**

- Start in Little India and take a look at all of the colorful streets and shops.
- Walk down to Kampong Glam - don't miss Sultan Masjid and grab an iced coffee from Selfie Coffee on Haji Lane.
- Stroll down Bugis Street and stop for a fruit juice.
- Find your way back to Chinatown & eat a cheap Michelin Star Meal!

♥ **DAY 3: AIRPORT**

- Eat at Maxwell Food Center
- Head to Changi Airport 4 hours before your fight.
- Explore

WEEKEND ITINERARY — BOUGIE

♥ DAY 1: MARINA BAY

- Fly into Changi Airport
- Check in to Marina Bay Sands
- Make your way to the rooftop pool immediately
- Have dinner at one of Marina Bay's Restaurants like CUT by Wolfgang Puck
- Stroll Marina Bay Sands– walk to Clarke Quay – take the river cruise.
- Head to the Lantern at Fullerton Bay for some cocktails with a great view.

♥ DAY 2: KAMPONG GLAM & MARINA BAY

- Start in Kampong Glam and grab breakfast at a cute cafe.
- Go to Orchard Road and get some shopping done!
- Back to Marina Bay to explore Gardens by the Bay
- Have an early dinner at Pollen and explore the Flower Dome
- Go to Clarke Quay to end your Singapore weekend with some fancy cocktails

♥ DAY 3: AIRPORT

- Head to Changi Airport 5 hours before your fight.
- Eat at Din Tai Fung
- Explore

5-DAY ITINERARY — BACKPACKER EXPERIENCE

♥ DAY 1: CHINATOWN & MARINA BAY

- Fly into Changi Airport
- Drop your stuff off at Beary Best Hostel in Chinatown
- Walk to Marina Bay
- Explore Marina Bay! Head towards the Helix Bridge and into The Shoppes @ Marina Bay for some air conditioning.
- Continue onto Gardens by the Bay - don't miss the supertrees (especially cool at night!).

♥ DAY 2: EXPLORE CHINATOWN

- Free Chinatown Walking Tour in the Morning
- Back to your hostel for some rest
- Maxwell Hawker Center and street beers for dinner

♥ DAY 3: KAMPONG GLAM

- Move to Beary Best Hostel in Kampong Glam
- Explore Kampong Glam - don't miss Sultan Masjid and grab an iced coffee from Selfie Coffee on Haji Lane.
- troll down Bugis Street and stop for a fruit juice.
- Get to Boon Tat Street at 6:57pm – for dinner

❤ DAY 4: LITTLE INDIA

- After breakfast, hop on the MRT towards Little India
- Explore the markets and try tea Indian-style
- Eat lunch in Tekka Center
- Join a Free Walking Tour in the afternoon (or morning, depending on the day)
- Find a little shop to do henna on your arm near Little India Arcade or Mustafa shopping center
- Have dinner at Khansama Tandoori Restaurant

❤ DAY 5: AIRPORT

- Have a kebab on Arab Street
- Head to the Airport 4 hours before your flight
- Explore

5-DAY ITINERARY - BOUGIE

❤ DAY 1: MARINA BAY

- Fly into Changi Airport
- Check in to Marina Bay Sands
- Make your way to the rooftop pool immediately
- Have dinner at one of Marina Bay's Restaurants like CUT by Wolfgang Puck

❤ DAY 2: KAMPONG GLAM & MARINA BAY

- Start in Kampong Glam and grab breakfast at a cute cafe.
- Check out the Sultan Mosque and Haji Lane
- Go to Orchard Road and get some shopping done!
- Have an early dinner at Pollen and explore the Flower Dome
- Go to Clarke Quay for some fancy cocktails

♥ DAY 3: SENTOSA

- Grab a taxi to Sentosa and have a spa day or a day at a beach club.
- End your day with dinner at Ce La Vie

♥ DAY 4: MARINA BAY

- Catch a view of Singapore from the Singapore Flyer (Ferris Wheel)
- Explore Gardens by the Bay
- Stroll Marina Bay Sands– walk to Clarke Quay – take the river cruise.
- Have lunch at Kinki
- Head to the Lantern at Fullerton Bay for some cocktails with a great view.
- Have dinner at One Altitude for a great view of the Bay.

♥ DAY 5: EXPLORE KAMPONG GLAM

- Enjoy your rooftop pool once more
- Head to Changi Airport 5 hours before your flight and explore JEWEL
- Eat at Din Tai Fung

PREPPING FOR SINGAPORE

VISAS

Good news - if you're coming from a Western country, including the EU, UK, Switzerland, Norway, the USA, Australia, or New Zealand: you're allowed to enter Singapore visa-free for 90 days. Canadians can enter Singapore visa-free for 30 days. You aren't permitted to do any business or to study - you're just there as a tourist!

That literally means, show up at the airport and they'll let you into the country by giving you a stamp in your passport.

BUT in order to enter Singapore – makes sure that you have at least 6 months of validity left in your passport. Some countries enforce this rule and some don't; Singapore does.

You need to have at least 6 months validity on your passport. For example, if it's January 1st, 2021, and your passport expires before June 1st, 2021 – Singapore will not allow you into the country.

PACKING LIST FOR SINGAPORE

Packing can be stressful, but the good news is this: Anything you forget at home can be replaced here in Singapore. Clothing, chargers, shoes, toiletries... there's no forgotten item that we can't find here.

That being said, by packing rule of thumb is this: If you're not sure if you need it...you probably don't need it. Pack light! The less you pack, the more free you are.

To help you narrow down what to bring and what to leave at home, here are my packing suggestions:

✔ A FLIGHT OUT

Or a train. Sometimes, Singaporean immigration wants to make sure you're not going to come into Singapore and stay forever – so, they want to see your flight out. Just have the confirmation on your phone and you're good. Don't have a flight out? Message me and I'll tell you how to get around the system!

✔ TRAVEL INSURANCE

Yes, you do need it. Everything from minor bouts of food poisoning to helicopter medevac off a mountain, a standard travel insurance policy is a nonnegotiable in my (literal) book.

World Nomads which offers full-coverage plans for extremely reasonable prices. Check out my website for official links.

✔ THE PERFECT SUITCASE

On a budget and plan on walking around the city & taking public transport? Carry a backpack. Coming with more cash and plan to take GrabTaxis? A rolley suitcase is fine for you.

The rolley suitcase I recommend is the Amazon Basics carry-on. It's actually very roomy!

However, I will be a backpack girl til the day I die – no matter how smooth the roads are. More specifically, the **Osprey Farpoint 55** or 40-liter bag.

- This bag qualifies as a carry-on
- It's extremely comfortable to wear
- The open-zip style means that you can keep your clothes organized
- I swear it's got Mary Poppins magic because I can fit 3-months of clothes in one tiny space

✔ WALKING SHOES

Bring 3 pairs of shoes

- ✔ 1 Pair of Flip Flops
- ✔ 1 Pair of Cute Walking Sandals
- ✔ 1 Pair of Hiking / Running Shoes

This is my official trifecta of shoes. Through rain, and on long sweaty walks, they've never failed me...and I still look cute. I replace the same pairs of shoes every year – find them in my travel store on my website.

✔ TRAVEL ADAPTER

Singapore uses type G plugs - the same as the UK. They also use 230 volts. If you're coming from the US, bring a converter with you. If you're coming from the UK, your voltage and plug is the same as Singapore's.

✔ PRESENTABLE CLOTHES

Unlike other parts of Asia, Singapore is a place where the "I've been traveling" elephant pants are a bit tacky and you won't be allowed in some dining or nightlife establishments without presentable attire.

✔ A SWEATER

Don't be fooled - even though Singapore is incredibly humid and hot, there's air conditioning everywhere and it's easy to get cold! A light sweater or a scarf that you can wrap around you will definitely come in handy.

✓ OB TAMPONS OR A MENSTRUAL CUP

You can find tampons over here, but they are more expensive and will have 1 option/style per store. Bring your own.

And if you've never used a menstrual cup, they are a game changer! Save money every month, go 12 hours with no leaks & swim with no drips. I prefer a menstrual cup on a long-haul flight…I just wish they called it something other than a "MENSTRUAL CUP".

✓ TROPICAL WEATHER MAKEUP

Humidity is no joke. Most foundations get super greasy and eyeshadows crease like it's their job. My makeup bag is pure perfection when it comes to long-lasting, humid, tropical weather products.

✓ QUICK DRY TOWEL

Hostel girls! Hostels usually don't provide towels so it's nice to bring a travel towel of your own. Not a total necessity, but a quick dry (usually some kind of microfiber) towel is nice to have- especially during rainy season when the heat isn't there to dry things quickly. Plus, it can double as your beach towel!

✓ EMERGENCY MONEY SOURCE/ $100 CASH US

Have a secret stash of cash or a backup credit card in case you get in a sticky situation. Keep this emergency money source separate from your other cards and cash- so that if you lose your wallet, you won't lose the secret stash, too.

✓ BANK CARDS

Travel with two cards – either 2 debit cards or 1 debit + 1 credit. In the case that your bank flags one card with fraudulent activity and disables it, you'll want to have a backup. If the machine eats a card, if a card gets stolen, or if you lose your purse on a night out, a backup card will make all the difference between having mom fly you home and you continuing your travels.

✓ YOUR PASSPORT!

Be like Santa and check it twice! Before you go to the airport, check and check again. To avoid catastrophes like this, get your free packing checklist on my website at TheSoloGirlsTravelGuide.com

✓ **EMPTY SPACE IN YOUR BAG**

It took me 5 years to learn that the less stuff you have, the more free you are. You are free to pick up and move around, free to shop for souvenirs, and free from relying on porters and taxis to help you carry your luggage. Plus, you're going to need space for all that extra shopping over here.

✗ **WHAT NOT TO PACK**

- Jeans
- High-heels
- Hairspray (ya won't use it)
- E-cigs/vape pens - they're illegal!
- A curling iron (with this humidity...no point)
- Too Many Bras (ya won't wear em')
- A Pharmacy of Medicine (you can get it all here)
- An "International Plan" for your cell phone data (your coverage will suck and it will be 5x more expensive – just get a local SIM card here when you land – your phone must be "unlocked")

BRINGING MEDICATION TO SINGAPORE

Singapore has some strict limitations when it comes to medicines and ingredients that you can bring into the country.

Prohibited OTC medicines:
- Any medicine containing Pseudoephedrine (a main ingredient in Actifed, Sudafed and Vicks inhalers), specifically any medicine containing over 10% of this ingredient.
- Any medicine containing Codeine

Other OTC medicines:

You can bring up to a 60-day supply of any non-prohibited OTC medicine, including vitamins.

Prohibited prescription medications:
- Opium
- Cannabis
- Amphetamines/ methamphetamines, including medications for the treatment of ADD/ADHD (Adderall, Vyvanse, Dexedrine)

Other prescription medications:

If your prescription includes a narcotic (morphine, oxycodone, hydrocodone), you may need to get advance permission from the Regional Bureau of Health and Welfare at least two weeks before your trip.

If your prescription includes a psychotropic (i.e. Valium), it will depend on the dosage of the active psychotropic ingredient. You can find the list of medicines in this category and the permitted dosages at **www.hsa.gov.sg/personal-medication**

For all permitted prescriptions, bring a copy of your prescription itself and keep the medication in its original bottle.

For more tips, articles, and packing guides—visit my blog at
▶ **TheSoloGirlsTravelGuide.com**

LET'S TALK ABOUT MONEY

Should you exchange a bunch of cash when you land or rely on the ATMs in Singapore?
Answer: A little bit of both.

Me? I use the ATMs because my bank (Charles Schwab) is designed for international travel with no ATM fees and great exchange rates. So, for frequent travelers, I suggest moving to my bank.

Otherwise, when going to a new country, I suggest traveling with $300 USD; $500 USD max (for theft reasons) and exchanging it at the airport. Rely on that for the first weekend.

Then, use the ATMs.

Here's a more detailed breakdown of how all of this works:

ATMS VS EXCHANGING CASH

ATM

If your bank gives you official Visa Exchange Rates and doesn't charge ATM fees or foreign transaction fees (like Chase or Charles Schwab), then ATM is the way to go.
When you land, look for a convenience store. Most will have an international ATM. Plan to take out about $100 to get you started.

EXCHANGE COUNTER

If your bank charges a high international rate, plan to exchange a decent amount of cash when you land in the airport. Bring about $500 in cash and exchange it for Singaporean Dollars.

> ☞ **PRO TIP**
> Don't exchange cash in America; wait until you land in Singapore.

The good news is that most everywhere accepts credit cards in Singapore, and that's what you should plan on using for hotels, restaurants, and even GrabTaxi (link your card to your account).

GET A TRAVEL CREDIT CARD

When to use a travel credit card

- Booking your flight
- Booking your hotels
- Booking tours online

Why use a travel credit card?

- Trip Protection! Be reimbursed for lost baggage, delayed flights ,and cancelled trips.
- Points, baby! Use this card to earn travel points on flights and hotels. Rack up enough points and you're ready to think business class flights and hotel upgrades!
- Lounge Access! Enjoy free alcohol, showers, and food in international airports.
- Purchase Protection! Example: I bought a 256 phone with my travel card, it was stolen in Indonesia, and my travel credit card reimbursed me fully.

💲 THE BEST TRAVEL CREDIT CARDS

- Chase Sapphire
- American Express Platinum
- Check out my blog for the full credit card breakdown: **https://thesologirlstravelguide.com/travel-credit-cards/**

FESTIVALS AND HOLIDAYS IN SINGAPORE

✸ JANUARY

JAN 25, 2020: CHINESE NEW YEAR (FEB 12, 2021)

- Chinese New Year is a big deal in Singapore. Of course, you'll head to Chinatown! Each year they have giant figures that represent the zodiac animal of the year - 2020 is the year of the rat, and 2021 is the year of the ox. There will be plenty going on in Chinatown and it's an incredibly lively time to visit.

✸ FEBRUARY

FEBRUARY 8, 2020: THAIPUSAM (JAN 28, 2021)

- This Tamil festival is celebrated on the day of the full moon during the Tamil month of Thai. Head over to Little India to see the festivities. Singapore is a great place to observe this holiday, as devotees who pierce their bodies and carry weight with the piercings are free to do so in Singapore, whereas in other countries, this practice has been banned.

✸ MAY

MAY 7, 2020: VESAK DAY (MAY 26, 2021)

- Vesak Day is observed by Buddhists to celebrate Buddha's birth, enlightenment, and death. You'll be able to see plenty of flowers, prayers, and blessings at Buddhist temples throughout Singapore.

MAY 24, 2020: HARI RAYA PUASA (MAY 13, 2021)

- Hari Raya Puasa is the celebration of the last day of Ramadan. There are lots of lights and tons of celebration in Kampong Glam.

✸ JULY

JULY 31, 2020: HARI RAYA HAJI

- Hari Raya Haji is the festival of sacrifice, when traditionally, Muslims would sacrifice an animal and pray. Head over to any mosque to see Hari Raya Haji being celebrated, however, you may not be allowed inside the mosque and may just have to observe from outside.

✸ AUGUST

AUGUST 9: NATIONAL DAY

- August 9, 1965 is when Singapore became an independent nation. Every day on National Day, there's a huge celebration all throughout Singapore. The air force will fly jets, fireworks will go off, and music is everywhere. The best place to observe National Day is in Marina Bay, in the heart of the action!

✸ NOVEMBER

NOVEMBER 14, 2020: DEEPAVALI/DIWALI (NOV 4, 2021)

- Diwali is the Hindu festival of lights and it celebrates lightness over darkness and good over evil. It's best celebrated in Little India, where there are incredible light displays and celebrations going on throughout the neighborhood.

DIRECTORY

Ambulance and Fire: 995
Ambulance (not an urgent emergency): 1777
Police (emergency): 999
Police (not urgent): 1800-225-0000
City Cab: +65 6555 1188

HOSPITALS

> **NOTE**
> It's hard to find a bad hospital in Singapore. Hospitals in this country are top-tier, care is high quality and costs are affordable! Here are just a few go-tos.

GLENEAGLE

⊕ **Where:** Near Orchard Road

⊕ **Address:** 6A Napier Road

❶ **Phone number:** +65 6473 7222

> **NOTE**
> More affordable

MOUNT ELIZABETH

🌐 **Where:** Directly Next to orchard road.

🌐 **Address:** 3 Mount Elizabeth

ℹ️ **Phone number:** +65 6250 0000
Make an appointment through WhatsApp: +65 8111 7777

> **NOTE**
> More expensive but has a reputable OBGYN and Children's Ward

THE OBGYN CENTRE - OBSTETRIC GYNAE

🌐 **Where:** Near Orchard Road

🌐 **Address:** 290 Orchard Road, in the Paragon Suites #11-07

ℹ️ **Phone number:** +65 6235 4188

> **NOTE**
> Best for reproductive surgeries, birth, c-section, and unwanted pregnancies

NOTE ON OBGYN SERVICES & UNWANTED PREGNANCIES

Girls, Singapore is so female-friendly and affordable. Singapore is one of the best medical tourism destinations for women. In other words, wait to address your reproductive needs until you get here!

Compare: My IUD in the US with amazing health-care coverage cost $900 USD. In Singapore, with no insurance, you can get an IUD starting at $70 USD. Shop around.

PS. I'm always loving to collect data on things like this. I'd love for you to message me and tell me about your medical tourism experience in Singapore!

• •

For more tips, articles, and packing guides—visit my blog at

▶ **TheSoloGirlsTravelGuide.com**

Always remember that you are braver than you think, stronger than you know, and smarter than you believe.

Coming to Singapore and have questions, want some tips or just want to chat about life in Asia?

Reach out to me on Instagram @**SoloGirlsTravelGuide**

No seriously. I'd love to hear from you and stalk your trip.

Did you love this book?
Help other girls find it by leaving a review on Amazon.

As a self-published author – doing this whole publishing thing by myself – reviews are what keeps this travel guide alive.

The True Story

OF HOW THE SOLO GIRL'S TRAVEL GUIDE WAS BORN

I was robbed in Cambodia.

Sure, the robber was a child and yes, I might have drunkenly put my purse down in the sand while flirting with an irresistible Swedish boy . . . but that doesn't change the fact that I found myself without cash, a debit card and hotel key at 1am in a foreign country.

My mini robbery, however, doesn't even begin to compare to my other travel misadventures. I've also been scammed to tears by taxi drivers, idiotically taken ecstasy in a country with the death penalty for drugs and missed my flight because how was I supposed to know that there are two international airports in Bangkok?

It's not that I'm a total idiot.
It's just that . . . people aren't born savvy travelers.

I'm not talking about hedonistic vacationers who spend their weekend at a resort sipping Mai Tais. I'm talking about train-taking, market-shopping, street food-eating travelers!

Traveling is not second (or third or fourth) nature; it's a skill that only comes with sweaty on-the-ground experience . . . especially for women!

In the beginning of my travels (aka the first 5 years), I made oodles of travel mistakes. And thank god I did. **These mistakes eventually turned me into the brilliant, resourceful, respected and established travel guru that I am today.**

A travel guru that was spawned through a series of being lost, hospitalized, embarrassed, and broke enough times to finally start learning from (and applying) her lessons.

Year-after-year and country-after-country, I started learning things like . . .

- Always check your hostel mattress for bed bugs.
- Local alcohol is usually toxic and will give you a hangover that lasts for days.
- The world isn't "touristy" once you stop traveling like a tourist.
- And most importantly, the best noodle shops are always hidden in back alleys.

After nearly 9 years of traveling solo around the world (4 continents and 20 countries, but who's counting?)—I travel like a god damn pro. I save money, sleep better, haggle harder, fly fancier, and speak foreign languages that help me almost almost blend in with the locals despite my blonde hair.

Yeah yeah yeah. I guess it's cool being a travel icon. But shoot . . .

Do you know how much money, how many panic attacks, and how many life—threatening risks I could have saved and/or avoided if only someone had freakin' queued me into all of this precious information along the way? A lot. A lotta' lot.

So, why didn't I just pick up a travel guide and start educating myself like an adult? *I had options . . . right?*

- I could've bought a copy of Lonely Planet . . . but how the hell am I supposed to smuggle a 1,500-page brick in my carry-on bag?
- Maybe Fodor's Travel Guides? No, I'm pretty sure the updated version doesn't include "How to Wash Your Travel Bra in the Sink".

- DK Eyewitness, perhaps? Hell no. I don't have 8 hours to sift through an encyclopedia and decode details relevant to my solo adventure.

There was no travel guide—not Lonely Planet, Fodor's or DK Eyewitness—that could've spared my tears or showed me how travel safer and smarter.

The book I needed didn't exist. So, I freaking wrote it myself.

What travel guide do you want me to write next?
Tell me on Instagram @SoloGirlsTravelGuide

Have any feedback? Love the book? Have a cool story? Want to see something in the book that isn't there? There's always room for love and improvement. Reach out to me and let me know!

Have any feedback?

Love the book?

Have a cool story?

Want to see something in the book that isn't there?

There's always room for love and improvement.
Reach out to me and let me know!

Send me your best photo from your trip in Singapore.
I feature the best ones on my social media every week!

Extra points if your travel guide is in the photo!

Alexa@TheSoloGirlsTravelGuide.com

Pass it On

Love the hell out of this book and then pass it on to the next travel queen.

Before you hop on a plane back home, find a girl traveling alone and give her the gift of badass, female empowered travel.

But first!

Leave your mark.

➡️

On the back cover, write your name, where you're from, when you traveled and if you have one, a travel tip to add to this book.

Oh and when you have inherited this book from a travel sister, take a picture! I'm dying to see it.

Tag me @SoloGirlsTravelGuide

xoxo, Alexa

Printed in Great Britain
by Amazon